Roman Britain Puzzles

Julian Morgan

The pictures used on the cover were kindly provided by
The Vindolanda Trust.

All other artwork used in this book was
created by the author.

Any errors or omissions in this book are
the fault of the author. They will be rectified
as soon as he becomes aware of them.

Please email with any requests for improvements
or corrections and if your suggestions are acted upon,
your name will be added on to the list on
the Acknowledgements page.

IN MEMORIAM

Erik de Geus

ACKNOWLEDGEMENTS

Special thanks go to Barbara Birley at the Vindolanda Trust
for her assistance in sourcing images and her enthusiasm
for this project along the way.

My thanks go to all who helped in checking
the manuscript of this book, especially
John Bird, Hugh Cooke and Uschi Cooke

CONTENTS

Introduction

My aim in writing this book has been to entertain and amuse those with an interest in the Romano-British treasures which surround us: so many signs of this former presence survive and we do well to remember that our country boasts some of the most exciting Roman archaeological finds in the world. Need I even mention the Vindolanda writing tablets? This new edition has been revised and expanded from the earlier one, during a period of lockdown-enforced introspection.

My own journeys through Roman Britain began properly in 1985 during my teacher training days. A fascination took hold of me then which has never abated: countless ex-students will attest to that, whom I have dragged round sites up and down the country and not least along Hadrian's Wall. The great cities of Bath, Chester and York still provide powerful testament to past times and below their streets the ancient structures can still be discerned. Every time I visit Limestone Corner I am unfailingly moved to see the scarred but still proud stones which once defeated the Roman legionaries: not much else stopped them here!

I have included a set of inscriptions of stones, all of which originate from Vindolanda. For the unfamiliar, there is an Epigraphy Appendix given and answers to the questions can be found in the Solutions section, where references are made to the Roman Inscriptions of Britain website. Don't be put off if you are new to inscriptions - they are a code in their own right and hugely rewarding to decipher. Where it comes to the names of historical people, I have tried to use commonly accepted spellings such as Boudicca, Cartimandua and Caratacus. It's hard to be confident whether these are really correct but you have to take a stand somewhere.

Please note that we publish a range of books for enthusiasts of Classics, Latin, Greek and the county of Yorkshire, which include lots of puzzles and poems. Please see our websites for further details:

www.j-progs.com and/or www.yorkshireauthor.com

Good luck with the puzzles and please email me if you see ways by which I can improve this book or if you have ideas about other new projects.

julian@j-progs.com

1   Around and about in Roman Britain

Complete the table below by filling in the names and by so doing, discover a concealed site running down the grid.

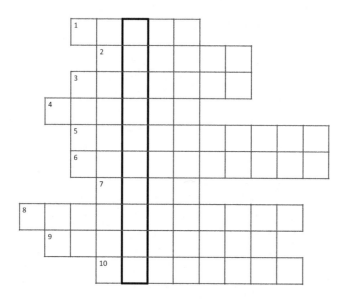

1. Drove once to see lighthouse on the cliffs (5)
2. Had to bring nothing to West Sussex villa with gladiator mosaics (6)
3. Saw green fort at Lindum (7)
4. Was calling for clash in Londinium (6)
5. Had to glue corset back to shape in Glevum (10)
6. Suffered lesser itch in abandoned Calleva (10)
7. Took a dip in Aquae Sulis (4)
8. Found secret nicer in Corinium (11)
9. Hit cowherd at Gloucestershire villa but I missed (9)
10. Upset crone with ale in legionary fort (8)

The concealed site is: ....

2   Hadrian's Wall sites

Hadrian's Wall is full of exciting places to discover. See if you can answer the questions below and finally solve the anagram which will lead you to one more of the sites.

Across

1. Cavalry fort near Chollerford sounds like a lot of horse races (8)
4. Can I bear a rebuilt fort? (6)
5. Solo turn at Housesteads provides relief (4)
7. Burnt on the turret? (7)
8. It's an appropriate-sounding place for building to stop (8)
12. Ices for motorists round Greatchesters fort (6)
13. and 9. Down Chug or lag about lake where soldiers once swam (4,5)
15. Stage changes for Roman portae (5)

Down

1. Drive van or car to the army museum (8)
2. South takes defences here (7)
3. There's an angle for limestone (6)
6. You can swap this fort for an old divan (10)
7. New bell for a Newcastle fort (7)
9. See 13. Across (5)
10. Carrawburgh temple has trim arrangement for eastern god (7)
11. Ditch bestrides rival lumps (6)
14. It's not a ridge in name and it's not made of metal (4)

One more Hadrian's Wall site is: ....

3 Wordsearch: British tribes

Britain was populated by different tribes before the Romans arrived and their identity was very important to the Celtic peoples. A set of their names has been listed below and then hidden in the grid: your job is to find them all. Words may go across, backwards, up, down or diagonally.

S	S	S	E	G	I	R	T	O	R	U	D	U	M	N
T	E	T	S	I	L	U	R	E	S	O	T	R	I	G
O	T	E	N	B	T	S	P	I	C	T	I	N	M	I
R	A	S	I	I	L	G	N	A	E	C	E	D	I	N
D	B	T	S	R	B	E	L	G	E	N	T	R	S	U
O	E	R	D	E	B	T	O	N	C	A	N	T	D	A
V	R	B	L	U	T	M	I	C	E	N	N	U	C	L
I	T	G	D	B	D	N	I	I	O	N	M	D	O	L
C	A	R	O	B	B	I	A	C	A	N	T	I	R	E
E	R	E	B	C	V	T	N	V	O	M	N	U	I	V
S	I	S	U	O	C	O	N	N	O	D	O	I	T	U
D	O	B	N	I	U	M	I	G	B	N	L	S	A	T
U	M	R	N	B	A	I	E	A	N	G	I	I	N	A
M	O	S	I	L	B	E	L	A	N	G	B	R	I	C
C	A	S	S	I	V	R	T	P	R	A	S	A	T	G
B	R	I	G	A	N	T	E	S	B	H	R	P	N	S

Atrebates	Cornovii	Iceni
Belgae	Deceangli	Ordovices
Brigantes	Dobunni	Parisi
Catuvellauni	Dumnonii	Silures
Coritani	Durotriges	Trinovantes

4   X marks the spot

See if you can fit the words listed into the grid below. One letter X has been done for you, to get you started.

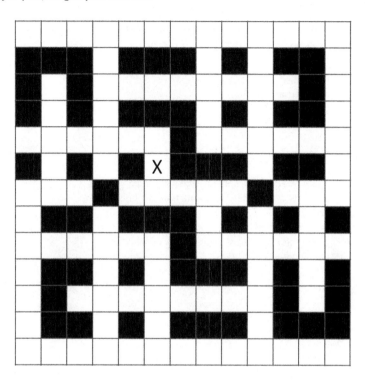

Three letters	Six letters	Seven letters
axe	Cantii	Olicana
egg	client	soldier
oil	Didius	
war	europa	*Eight letters*
	Gallus	
Five letters	insula	Boulogne
	Medusa	drainage
aquae	pagans	
Aulus		*Thirteen letters*
Ceres		
Iceni		altars of stone
tunic		Hardknott Pass

5   Issues of occupation

There are three parts to this quiz. First, you should identify the answer to each of the first questions of the pairs below. Then, answer the second questions of each pair with a number. Finally, put the first letters of your first answers in the descending order of the list of numbers (with high numbers first) to reveal a part of the occupation process.

1. On which island, called Mona by the Romans, did the Druids perform their rituals? (8) ....
   Approximately how far in miles did Suetonius Paulinus have to travel from this island to face Boudicca's rebels in London? ....

2. Which governor of Britain was made famous forever by his son-in-law's history book? (8) ....
   For how many years did he serve as governor in Britain? ....

3. Which birds were regarded by the Romans as symbols of their legions? (6) ....
   How many of these birds were associated with each legion? ....

4. Which Roman town, known as Verulamium, was sacked by Boudicca during her revolt? (2,6) ....
   According to the Annals of Tacitus, how many rebellious Britons were killed by the Romans in the final battle of the revolt? ....

5. Which modern city, known to the Romans as Isca Dumnoniorum, can be found at the southern end of the Fosse Way? (6) ....
   In which year AD was this road established as frontier system? ....

6. Boudicca was Queen of the Iceni - but which other tribe took a leading part in her revolt of AD 60? (11) ....
   It seems a very low number - but how many Romans did Tacitus claim had died in the final battle against Boudicca? ....

7. What sort of building was dedicated to Claudius in Colchester during the early part of the Occupation? (6) ....
   How many legions had Claudius sent to conquer the island? ....

8. What name is given to the famous war which Julius Caesar fought in France and Britain? (6) ....
   For how many years did this war last? ....

9. During which Roman emperor's reign did the revolt of Boudicca happen? (4) ....
   In which year AD was this? ....

The part of the process was:

6   Inscriptions I

See how much you know about abbreviations and letters used in Roman inscriptions. By answering the questions and then inserting the first letters of each answer into the grid below, you should reveal something the inscriptions have in common. In case you don't know much at all about this material, you should refer to the Epigraphy Appendix at the back of this book, which will help you out.

1. These three letters were commonly used to mean a *cohort*.   ....
2. These three letters were used on gravestones to mean *years*.   ....
3. This letter was used as an abbreviation for the name *Rufus*.   ....
4. These three letters were used on gravestones to mean *he* or *she lived*.   ....
5. In the abbreviation HSE, this letter stood for the Latin word meaning *is*.   ....
6. This letter was used as an abbreviation on gravestones to mean *days*.   ....
7. This letter was used as an abbreviation on altars to mean for *Jupiter*.   ....
8. These three letters were used as an abbreviation to mean *for the spirit*.   ....
9. In the abbreviation HSE, this letter was used to mean *buried*.   ....
10. This letter was used as an abbreviation for the name *Titus*.   ....
11. These three letters were used to refer to an assistant centurion.   ....
12. This two letter abbreviation stood for a word which meant *born*.   ....
13. This two letter Latin word meant *and*.   ....

What the inscriptions have in common is:

1	2	3	4	5	6	7	8	9	.	10	11	12	13

In this stone, what can we learn about Celer?

....

7

7   Brigantes sudoku

You know how sudoku works. All you have to do is to place numbers one to nine in each vertical and horizontal line and then make sure that each number appears once in each of the nine 3x3 squares. The difference here is that this is Brigantes sudoku! Instead of numbers, you need to insert each letter of the northern tribe in the same way. Good luck.

	S		I					
E					B	G		R
		I		T		A		
		T		A			S	B
	R	N		I				
B	A			G		T		I
		A					N	
	I	G			T			E
	T		E	S	R		G	A

In this stone, can you identify the soldier mentioned and his rank?

....

8 Wordsearch plus: now and then

There are two parts to this puzzle, which features a set of locations in Roman Britain. First off, you should try to match the modern place names on the left with their Latin names on the right in the lists below.

Bath	*Aquae Sulis*
Carlisle	*Arbeia*
Chester	*Calleva Atrebatum*
Cirencester	*Camulodunum*
Colchester	*Corinium*
Dover	*Deva*
Exeter	*Dubris*
Gloucester	*Eboracum*
Lincoln	*Glevum*
London	*Isca Dumnoniorum*
Silchester	*Lindum*
South Shields	*Londinium*
St Albans	*Luguvalium*
York	*Verulamium*

And now to the grid, where you should find the Latin place names all hidden away. Words may go across, backwards, up, down or diagonally.

E	L	M	U	R	O	I	N	O	N	M	U	D	A	C	S	I	S
B	U	E	D	E	V	A	V	L	G	L	E	V	U	M	U	I	S
O	G	R	B	A	V	R	Q	E	A	T	R	E	B	I	N	L	I
R	U	T	E	O	C	A	M	U	L	O	D	U	N	U	M	O	R
T	V	H	R	E	R	L	U	G	A	I	E	B	R	A	U	N	B
C	A	L	L	E	V	A	A	T	R	E	B	A	T	U	M	D	U
S	L	D	V	E	C	E	C	L	U	I	S	A	Q	T	L	I	D
I	I	R	U	B	L	A	Q	U	A	E	M	U	D	N	I	L	N
M	U	I	N	I	R	O	C	R	M	E	N	N	L	U	G	O	O
L	M	U	E	V	E	R	U	L	A	M	I	U	M	I	I	U	L
R	E	M	U	I	N	I	D	N	O	L	I	N	D	A	S	P	B

9   Out and about in Roman Britain

Test yourself out on your general knowledge of our Romano-British heritage.

Across

6. This kind of people were the original inhabitants (6)
7. Chopping tools (4)
8. The legionary soldier always had to carry his (3)
9. It needed trimming in an oil lamp (4)
10. Ages of occupation (4)
12. It's the location of the Vindolanda Museum (11)
16. Caracalla's much-damaged brother (4)
19. Home county of Maiden Castle (6)
20. Animal's mark seen in roof tiles (3)
21. Containers of clay (4)
22. Street linking Fosse Way to Watling Street near St Albans (6)

Down

1. It's what leather goods at Vindolanda did not always do (6)
2. Upright parts of a palisade (6)
3. This ancient road ran from Norfolk to Wiltshire (8,3)
4. Porta (4)
5. Chester (4)
11. Second part of an early Christian emblem made up of two Greek letters (3)
13. Something a Roman would do in a triclinium (3)
14. Animals kept by equites (6)
15. Discretion shown officially to promote Romanisation (6)
17. AKA Cupid (4)
18. Rounded recess in a wall (4)

10   Cryptic Roman Britain

See if you can solve these tricky clues.

Across

1. Pharos emission (5)
4. Drove around Dubris (5)
7. Roman pride in the first person (3)
8. It's a job for the lanista to do (5)
9. No mud around the burial (5)
10. Doubting inside the mines (3)
11. Missing from York (5)
14. Apparent change in religion (5)
17. Donate a cent for Ermine Street Guard's job (5)
20. Don't take dagger first to defend (5)
23. Bloody sprouts with Mithras (3)
24. A rum do after lightweight start? That's fishy! (5)
25. Goes direct to Anglesey? I mean! (5)
26. Steak and kidney recalls road to Colchester (3)
27. Secure victory in Roman plan for Boudicca (5)
28. Groovy ceilings counteracted (5)

Down

1. New territory tongue (5)
2. A grin to match horreum inside (5)
3. Last cohort in the legion? (5)
4. Empress Julia's second (5)
5. No pole under Colchester Castle (5)
6. Read EQES on his grave (5)
12. It's no sin to remove the map where you change your horse (3)
13. A head start for Claudius (3)
15. Short soldiers for graves (3)
16. Greeting in the waves (3)
17. Confused legate doesn't have time for bird (5)
18. I argue coins aren't general (5)
19. Try to lure the locals (5)
20. No aspiration for hurt fighting forces? (5)
21. Clever sounding spirits of places (5)
22. Destroys Romano-British leftovers (5)

11   What have the Romans ever done for us?

Complete the grid below by filling in some of the advantages which the invaders brought to Britain and discover a name for the process they had in common running down the grid.

1. Great places of entertainment such as the one at St Albans (8)
2. Transport links such as the Fosse Way or Watling Street (5)
3. Containers for oil and other liquid foodstuffs (8)
4. Artworks made of small pieces for floors and walls (7)
5. Coloured murals (13)
6. Large, well-equipped houses which often served estates around them (6)
7. Distance markers on major routes (10)
8. Places to wash and relax (5)
9. Carved figures to adorn hallways and porticoes (7)
10. Teaching and learning for young people's improvement (9)
11. Underfloor heating systems (10)
12. An alcoholic drink made from grapes (4)

The process in common to all these advantages is known as : ....

12   Romano-British roads

See if you can answer the clues below, which all relate to the road network in Roman Britain. Then try to identify a feature of the Roman roads by solving the anagram made by the letters in the shaded squares.

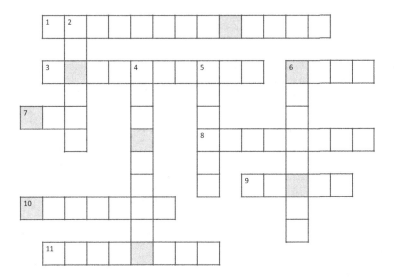

Across

1. Twister tangle for Dover Chester route (7,6)
3. Red tree set to lead North from York (4,6)
6. North Yorkshire Wheeldale location could tie you up (4)
7. Roman road seen in deviation (3)
8. Seek link with dice to find way from Dorset to Norfolk (8)
9. Find a nest in tatters on Chichester London street (5)
10. It's an apparent harbour route from Salisbury to Silchester (7)
11. Sway foes en route from Exeter to Lincoln (5,3)

Down

2. Make an effort in way from Cirencester to St Albans (6)
4. Agents take tea along early northern frontier (9)
5. Firemen weren't so loud on street to Lincoln (6)
6. There's a kind of precision for route along the wall (8)

A feature of the Roman roads is: ....

13   Wordsearch: Roman Britons

We know the identities of various individuals whose origins were from Britain. See if you can find them where they have been hidden in the grid below. Words may go across, backwards, up, down or diagonally.

T	C	A	R	T	B	O	U	D	I	C	C	A	N	N
A	A	A	H	B	P	S	U	I	S	A	T	O	G	O
S	L	C	S	U	I	U	M	M	O	R	N	L	N	P
P	B	C	U	S	V	N	C	O	M	A	S	G	I	R
R	A	A	N	U	I	A	R	T	I	T	A	C	L	A
A	N	L	M	N	B	V	V	I	U	A	N	T	E	S
S	U	G	U	B	N	O	E	R	L	C	U	N	B	C
U	T	A	D	U	N	I	N	L	T	U	I	C	O	N
T	I	C	O	D	I	C	U	L	L	S	V	M	N	I
A	U	U	G	I	T	S	T	A	T	A	M	R	U	U
G	S	S	O	G	I	A	I	N	N	I	U	R	C	S
U	C	O	T	O	N	T	U	U	U	M	M	N	I	A
S	O	D	I	C	C	A	S	S	B	O	U	D	U	R
C	A	R	T	I	M	A	N	D	U	A	R	T	B	S
S	U	I	M	M	O	C	N	I	T	I	N	C	O	U
T	A	S	C	D	R	U	I	D	S	I	O	V	A	T

Alban	Cassivellaunus	Prasutagus
Boudicca	Cogidubnus	Tasciovanus
Calgacus	Commius	Tincommius
Caratacus	Cunobelin	Togodumnus
Cartimandua	Druids	Venutius

14   Numbers on the wall

*The object of the puzzle is to find out which letter of the alphabet is represented by each of the 22 numbers used. You are given one full word to start you off, so you can begin by entering the letters from this wherever their numbers appear in the grid. Each word you make should be connected somehow to Hadrian's Wall. As you decode each letter, write it in the **Letters deciphered** table and cross it off in the **Letters used** table.*

1 F	2 O	3 R	4 T									
6	20	4	11	5								
22	17	9	9	8	7							
4	8	3	3	12	4							
18	3	17	13	17	3	10						
18	17	4	12	19	17	10						
9	17	4	3	20	13	12	14					
15	17	3	3	17	11	16	14					
21	3	20	13	11	20	21	20	17				
7	20	9	12	11	17	14	4	9	12			
21	3	17	12	4	2	3	20	8	7			
7	20	9	20	4	17	3	10		3	2	17	6

Letters deciphered

1	2	3	4	5	6	7	8	9	10	11	12	13	14	15	16	17	18	19	20	21	22
F	O	R	T																		

Letters used

A	B	C	D	E	F̶	G	H	I	K	L	M	N	O̶	P	R̶	S	T̶	U	V	W	Y

15

15   A work of art

Solve this riddle by answering all the statements which follow. As you answer each question, insert a letter in the grid below, where you will see an answer forming which represents a high point of achievement in Romano-British art.

1.   My first is in baths but not in Bath.
2.   My second is in cohort but not Coritani.
3.   My third is in Aquae and also Iceni.
4.   My fourth is a triple in Lullingstone.
5.   My fifth is in Letocetum and also in Wall.
6.   My sixth is in Mithras and also in Medway.
7.   My seventh is in Londinium but never in Lindum.
8.   Silures have twice my eighth.
9.   My ninth is in Deva but not in Ordovices.
10.   My tenth is in Sulis but absent from Sul.
11.   My eleventh is held twice by Caratacus and Caracalla.

The Roman thing is:

1	2	3	4	5	6	7	8	9	10	11

To which goddess, representing whom, was this stone dedicated?

....

What was the name of the person who had it made?

....

From which part of the Roman Empire did he come?

....

In which legion did he serve?

....

16   Inscriptions II

See how much you know about abbreviations and letters used in Roman inscriptions. By answering the questions and then inserting the first letters of each answer into the grid below, you should reveal something the inscriptions have in common. In case you don't know much at all about this material, you should refer to the Epigraphy Appendix at the back of this book, which will help you out.

1. This letter was often used on gravestones to mean *months*.   ....

2. These three letters were often used as an abbreviation for *Augustus*.   ....

3. These two letters at the top of a gravestone meant *for the spirits of the departed*.   ....

4. These two letters give us a word which meant *out of* or *from*.   ....

5. These three letters were often used as an abbreviation for *Tiberius*.   ....

6. This was the second letter of three in the title *to Jupiter, Best and Greatest*.   ....

7. These three letters were often used as an abbreviation for *Legion*.   ....

8. This letter was used as an abbreviation for the name *Aulus*.   ....

9. This letter was used as an abbreviation for the *Senate*.   ....

10. These four letters were often used as an abbreviation for a *tribune*.   ....

What the inscriptions have in common is:

1	2	3	4	5	6	7	8	9	10

In this inscription, which military unit is referred to and how is it described?

....

Why do you think there is a boar shown here?

....

17   Legionary sudoku

You know how sudoku works. All you have to do is to place numbers one to nine in each vertical and horizontal line and then make sure that each number appears once in each of the nine 3x3 squares. The difference here is that this is Legionary sudoku! Instead of numbers, you need to insert each letter of the Roman soldier in the same way. Good luck.

	G		I	R				Y
R				N	Y	L		
	O	N	A			E		I
A		R		O			L	N
		L	R		I		Y	
O	E			L	G		I	
	Y	O		I			N	L
		A	O	E		Y		
		R	G			A	I	E

What do you think was the purpose of this stone?

....

18 Wordsearch plus: where's that?

There are two parts to this puzzle, which showcases different Roman constructions and where you can find them in Britain. First off, you should try to match the items on the left with the places they may belong to on the right in the lists below.

Amphitheatre	Bath
Civilian vicus	Caerleon
Fort reconstruction	Chester
Great Bath	Chesters
Latrine block	Colchester
Legionary barracks	Dover
Lighthouse	Fishbourne
Military bath house	Housesteads
Mithraeum	London
Multangular tower	South Shields
Old Work	St Albans
Palace	Vindolanda
Temple of Claudius	Wroxeter
Theatre	York

And now to the grid, where you should find the place names all hidden away. Words may go across, backwards, up, down or diagonally.

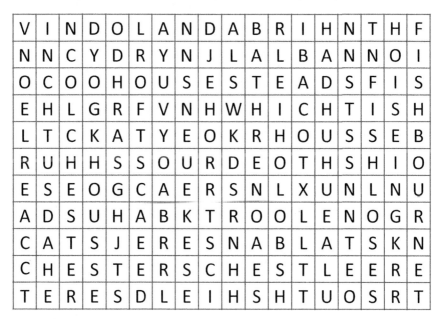

V	I	N	D	O	L	A	N	D	A	B	R	I	H	N	T	H	F
N	N	C	Y	D	R	Y	N	J	L	A	L	B	A	N	N	O	I
O	C	O	O	H	O	U	S	E	S	T	E	A	D	S	F	I	S
E	H	L	G	R	F	V	N	H	W	H	I	C	H	T	I	S	H
L	T	C	K	A	T	Y	E	O	K	R	H	O	U	S	S	E	B
R	U	H	H	S	S	O	U	R	D	E	O	T	H	S	H	I	O
E	S	E	O	G	C	A	E	R	S	N	L	X	U	N	L	N	U
A	D	S	U	H	A	B	K	T	R	O	O	L	E	N	O	G	R
C	A	T	S	J	E	R	E	S	N	A	B	L	A	T	S	K	N
C	H	E	S	T	E	R	S	C	H	E	S	T	L	E	E	R	E
T	E	R	E	S	D	L	E	I	H	S	H	T	U	O	S	R	T

19   Out and about in Roman Britain

Test yourself out on your general knowledge of our Romano-British heritage.

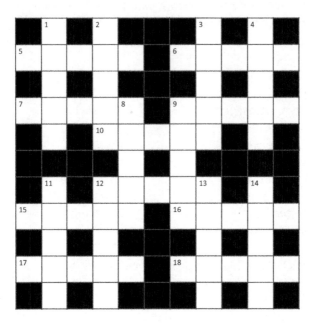

Across

5. Leicester (5)
6. Insula or barracks? (5)
7. Verulamium saint (5)
9. Main material for building of Hadrian's Wall (5)
10. Receptacle for clothing in a bath house (5)
12. Cavalryman's mount (5)
15. Solway water (5)
16. Type of shore fort (5)
17. Incomplete remains (5)
18. Soothsayer with an eye for the birds (5)

Down

1. Legionary bird (5)
2. Celtic belief system (5)
3. Roofing material (5)
4. Boudicca's tribe (5)
8. York-based legion which went missing (5)
9. Vindolanda caligae (5)
11. Repairable javelin (5)
12. Street from London to Chichester (5)
13. Doncaster (5)
14. Bowl-shaped altar top (5)

20   Cryptic Roman Britain

See if you can solve these tricky clues.

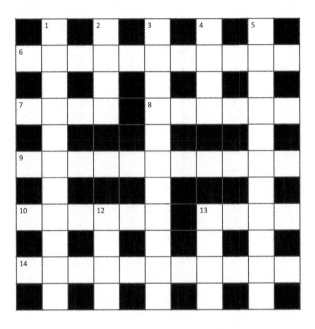

Across

6. Sound inputs for non-legionary soldiers (11)
7. A lion's prey in St Albans or Corbridge (4)
8. Twenty short of century complement? (6)
9. Exude vacant look for a virgin site (11)
10. The interval's torture, with nothing left out! (6)
13. It's round at Birdoswald (4)
14. Test man belt along the top of the wall (11)

Down

1. All run gamut of oddly-shaped tower (11)
2. Boudicca's no substitute for him (4)
3. Distance keeps about thirty watchmen in these (11)
4. Rock by Lough in Northumberland (4)
5. Nettle stems for vici (11)
12. Star turns kept out by granary supports (4)
13. Celtic pulling power (4)

21   Women of Roman Britain

It is a pity but we don't have all that many names of women who lived in Roman Britain. See how many you can fill below and by so doing, discover something which connects them running down the grid.

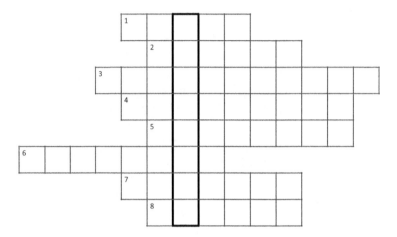

1.   Confuse nomad for Septimius Severus' wife Julia (5)

2.   Take a basin for Hadrian's wife (6)

3.   A tunic drama for the Brigantian queen (11)

4.   Lucky-sounding Julia from Sardinia lived with her husband in York, no truant oaf (9)

5.   Do basic cut with lost holy man to find famous Iceni queen (8)

6.   Sulpicia from Vindolanda suffered idle pain (8)

7.   Second name Severa, she could have been in Strictly (7)

8.   South Shields *Queenie* is still resplendent in gear (6)

Something which connects them was: ....

22   Taking directions

Test yourself out and see if you can fill in the gaps in the table below. All the clues are on the grid.

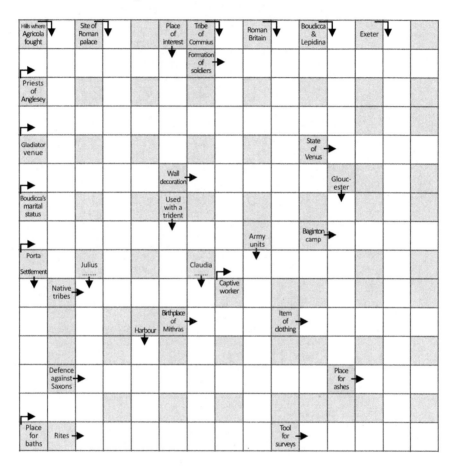

23 Wordsearch: the occupation

See if you can find the people and places which played their various parts during the occupation of Roman Britain. They have been listed below and then hidden in the grid. Words may go across, backwards, up, down or diagonally.

E	G	O	C	O	G	I	D	U	B	N	U	S	I	R
M	A	S	N	A	B	L	A	T	S	A	T	R	E	O
P	P	U	N	L	Y	R	O	C	H	E	S	T	E	R
E	S	C	L	O	N	D	O	N	I	U	S	O	T	H
R	E	A	P	U	A	T	I	U	S	E	V	G	E	G
O	T	T	A	R	S	U	S	S	H	L	O	O	A	U
R	N	A	R	B	I	P	K	C	H	E	S	D	T	O
C	A	R	I	R	I	B	L	B	A	N	S	U	R	R
L	V	A	S	I	I	O	U	A	U	L	P	M	E	O
A	O	C	I	A	C	C	I	D	U	O	B	N	B	B
U	N	R	O	C	E	S	T	E	V	T	N	U	A	H
D	I	S	L	I	N	U	B	A	N	E	I	S	T	C
I	R	O	F	O	I	S	S	E	L	T	R	U	E	I
U	T	L	F	O	S	S	E	W	A	Y	O	I	S	R
S	U	S	S	I	C	R	A	N	A	R	C	I	C	S
M	R	I	V	E	R	M	E	D	W	A	Y	S	T	A

Atrebates	Emperor Claudius	River Medway
Aulus Plautius	Fosse Way	Rochester
Boudicca	Iceni	St Albans
Caratacus	London	Togodumnus
Cogidubnus	Narcissus	Trinovantes
Colchester	Richborough	Verica

24   Steel yourself

Try to fit the words listed below into the grid. One of them has been done for you, to get you started.

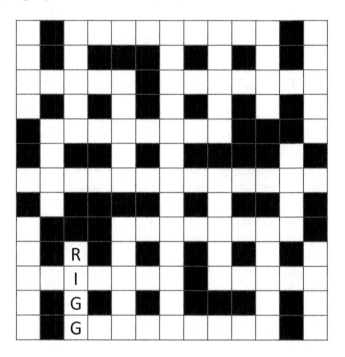

Four letters	Five letters (cont'd)	Eight letters
berm	Coria	Antonine
Dere	Fosse	javelins
huts	Iceni	
jury	lance	*Nine letters*
lead	ninth	
~~Rigg~~	races	*Chedworth*
		Great Bath
Five letters	*Seven letters*	
		Thirteen letters
altar	tribune	
aquae	Tacitus	*Watling Street*
annal		*writing tablet*
aurei		

25   Army matters

There are three parts to this quiz. First, you should identify the answer to each of the first questions of the pairs below, which are rather cryptic in places. Then, answer the second questions of each pair with a number. Finally, put the first letters of your first answers in the ascending order of the list of numbers (with low numbers first) to reveal a special place for soldiers.

1. Mirth as soldiers' god appears in Carrawburgh
    and London. (7)   ....
    In which century AD did the worship of this god
    first start to appear?   ....

2. Later northern wall's not inane. (8)   ....
    How long in miles was this wall?   ....

3. Stoat takes street from London to Lincoln. (6)   ....
    For approximately how many days did the
    Romans occupy Britain? Go on, have a guess!   ....

4. Our men take cab from the North to Roman fort
    at York. (8)   ....
    Which legion first built the fort there?   ....

5. Upset? So torch these units! (7)   ....
    How many of these units were there in a legion?   ....

6. It could be nice if not so loud for Romans'
    enemies. (5)   ....
    How many daughters did Prasutagus and
    Boudicca have?   ....

7. Get ale for this senior army commander. (6)   ....
    Approximately how many men were there in a legion?   ....

8. Set up a road sign for unit to protect. (8)   ....
    How many centurions were there in a legion?   ....

9. Lines go about as soldiers form groups. (7)   ....
    How many years did it take the Romans to build
    the Fosse Way, after the first invasion of AD 43?   ....

10. He's a sort of turbine in charge. (7)   ....
    How many men were there in a century?   ....

A special place for soldiers was:

26   Inscriptions III

See how much you know about abbreviations and letters used in Roman inscriptions. By answering the questions and then inserting the first letters of each answer into the grid below, you should reveal something the inscriptions have in common. In case you don't know much at all about this material, you should refer to the Epigraphy Appendix at the back of this book, which will help you out.

1. These two words meant *from a vision (or dream)*.   ....
2. These three letters were used as an abbreviation for *power* or *rank*.   ....
3. These three letters were often used as an abbreviation for *Emperor*.   ....
4. This letter was used as an abbreviation for the name *Gaius*.   ....
5. This letter was used as an abbreviation to mean *Roman* or *from Rome*.   ....
6. These two letters form a word which meant *to* or *towards*.   ....
7. These two letters were used to indicate that someone had been a *commander*.   ....
8. These three letters were used as an abbreviation to mean *is buried here*.   ....
9. These four letters were used on gravestones to mean *years of service*.   ....

What the inscriptions have in common is:

1	2	3	4	5	6	7	8	9

What was the purpose of this stone?

....

To which god was it dedicated?

....

What do the letters L M suggest at the end?

....

27 Romanised sudoku

You know how sudoku works. All you have to do is to place numbers one to nine in each vertical and horizontal line and then make sure that each number appears once in each of the nine 3x3 squares. The difference here is that this sudoku has been Romanised! You have to use the nine letters of this process in the same way. Good luck.

	O		D	I		N		
	A	S	N			I		D
		D		S			M	O
	M			E		S		
N		E	I	A	D			M
D		O			S	E		A
O				N		D		
S	D			M	R		A	
	R						I	E

What do you think was the purpose of this stone and who had it made?

....

28   Wordsearch plus: who's who

There are two parts to this puzzle, which features different named individuals in Romano-British history. First off, you should try to match the descriptors on the left with the names on the right in the lists below.

Brigantian chief captured and sent to Rome	Agricola
Emperor who died in York in AD 211	Aulus Plautius
Emperor who occupied Britain in AD 43	Boudicca
Emperor whose wall ran from the Solway Firth to the River	Caratacus
Empress who accompanied her husband to Britain in AD	Cartimandua
First governor of Roman Britain	Claudius
General who led the early invasions of 55 and 54 BC	Commius
Governor who campaigned in northern Britain from AD 78	Constantine
Governor who suppressed a major revolt in AD 60	Hadrian
King of the Atrebates	Julius Caesar
Proclaimed emperor in York in AD 306	Sabina
Queen of the Brigantes	Septimius
Queen of the Iceni	Suetonius
Wife of Flavius Cerealis	Sulpicia Lepidina

And now to the grid, where you should find the names of the individuals all hidden away. Words may go across, backwards, up, down or diagonally.

J	U	L	I	A	A	G	R	I	C	O	L	A	C	L	A	U	D
U	N	S	U	R	E	V	E	S	S	U	I	M	I	T	P	E	S
L	S	U	E	T	O	N	I	U	S	P	A	U	L	I	N	U	S
I	F	B	M	E	N	I	T	N	A	T	S	N	O	C	L	A	U
U	D	I	U	S	A	U	L	U	S	B	R	I	G	A	N	T	I
S	G	G	I	N	M	M	I	C	O	M	M	I	U	S	I	N	D
C	B	B	I	S	U	I	T	U	A	L	P	S	U	L	U	A	U
A	S	B	U	S	A	U	D	N	A	M	I	T	R	A	C	E	A
E	A	I	S	U	S	I	C	H	A	D	R	I	A	N	U	S	L
S	U	L	P	I	C	I	A	L	E	P	I	D	I	N	A	A	C
A	R	U	I	C	A	R	A	C	T	A	N	O	C	C	A	R	T
R	S	C	A	R	A	T	A	C	U	S	U	L	P	C	O	L	A

29   Out and about in Roman Britain

Test yourself out on your general knowledge of our Romano-British heritage.

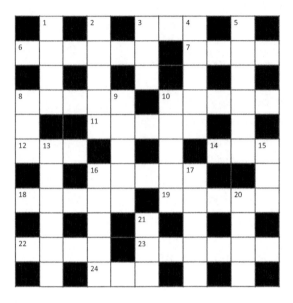

Across

3. Affliction for Emperor Claudius (3)
6. Rebuilt fort at South Shields (6)
7. Shield boss (4)
8. Tower at each corner of the fort (5)
10. Boudicca's status after Prasutagus' departure (5)
11. A contubernium, perhaps (5)
12. Heavy pole for battering (3)
14. Origin of Mithras' birth (3)
16. Corn goddess (5)
18. Bowl-shaped altar top (5)
19. Animals kept for their wool (5)
22. Native British inhabitant (4)
23. Soft metal mined in North West England and Wales (6)
24. What you might do in the King's Bath (3)

Down

1. Widely used metal (4)
2. Sources of water in villas and forts (5)
3. Roman levy on the locals (3)
4. Attendant for Venus (5)
5. Common shape of a Roman fort (6)
8. Hot under the floor (3)
9. Cavalryman (5)
10. Home of the Ordovices and the Silures (5)
13. Types of building in a vicus (6)
15. On Hadrian's Wall, Milking ... (3)
16. Belief systems (5)
17. Transports (5)
20. Enamel insertions in statue heads (4)
21. What you'd do in the Odeon, perhaps (3)

30   Cryptic Roman Britain
See if you can solve these tricky clues.

1		2			3			4		5
	■		■			■		■		
6					■		7			
	■		■	8		9			■	
	■		10				11		■	
12					■	13				
	■		14		15				■	
	■	16		■	17			■	18	
19				■		■	20			
	■		■		■			■		
21										

Across

1. Spy garlic at St Albans shows? (6,5)
6. That's what it is called in Exeter (4)
7. Box flues send time out (4)
8. By way of the road (3)
10. Evil lady goes in the house (5)
12. Cut in garb (5)
13. Chi-Rho reading matter (5)
14. Rustic location for villa (5)
17. Claudius' Britannicus (3)
19. Coax essayist to find tools inside (4)
20. King of Corbridge, maybe (4)
21. Years shoot by in a second for fortune tellers (11)

Down

1. Stole its tea so there's none left in Housesteads loo block (6,5)
2. Reach out East for support (4)
3. It's a polite sort of law for the non-military Roman (5)
4. Equips below shoulders (4)
5. Make agreements beyond fort walls (11)
8. Cruel loss of ten in village (5)
9. Verulamium saint in final ban (5)
10. Half courage for Roman man (3)
11. You might do in Aquae Sulis (3)
15. Soar down straight ways (5)
16. Boudicca's imperial foe (4)
18. Stones or castles - the gap's the same (4)

31   Tribal disorder

Complete the grid below by solving the anagrams and filling in the answers, which are all names of British tribes. Then you will reveal the name of another tribe running down the grid.

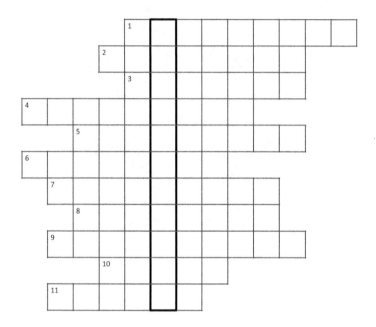

1.   Battersea
2.   Air tonic
3.   Is rules
4.   Nags tribe
5.   Score void
6.   I con Ivor
7.   Nice glade
8.   Mid union
9.   Or used grit
10. In ice
11. Is pair

The tribe going down the grid is: ....

32   Commodities

Britain was an important trading partner for Rome, which was a factor into why they first came here. Put your solutions in the grid below and then try to solve the anagram made by the letters in the shaded squares, which refers to something crucial to Romano-British trade.

Across

1. This metal was mined in Cornwall. (3)
2. These factories made containers and vessels for daily use. (9)
5. These shellfish were popular on Romano-British dining tables. (7)
7. This natural material was used to make Roman togas, amongst other articles of clothing. (4)
9. These metalworkers might have seen Vulcan as their special god. (6)
12. This popular drink would have mostly been imported from warmer lands. (4)
13. This precious metal was mined in South Wales. (4)
14. These animals were the source of 7. Across. (5)
12. These sweet fruits were dried and brought to Britain from warmer climes. (5)

Down

1. Animal hides were turned into leather in these places. (9)
3. These natural resources equipped the Roman soldiers for building palisade walls. (5)
4. These transports of the day facilitated both the import and export trades. (5)
6. This precious metal was used for tableware and jewellery. (6)
8. This fruit was essential in making imported oil. (5)
10. This squared-off bar permitted easy transportation and storage of valuable metal. (5)
11. These were the places in 1. Down where goods were stored. (5)

Something crucial to Romano-British trade was: ....

33   Wordsearch: towns in Latin

Roman Britain's towns all had Latin names once. Various of them have been listed below and then hidden in the grid: your job is to find them. Words may go across, backwards, up, down or diagonally.

C	A	S	T	R	I	S	E	L	K	W	D	E	V	A
O	H	M	U	R	O	D	O	T	C	A	L	I	Q	N
R	O	M	Q	U	R	T	V	E	R	M	C	U	N	L
M	U	M	U	N	U	D	O	L	U	M	A	C	O	L
I	U	R	A	D	N	C	L	I	N	E	L	R	V	V
N	I	I	E	R	N	A	N	E	S	S	L	K	I	E
I	I	L	M	U	I	I	M	U	G	L	E	R	O	N
U	M	C	I	A	R	V	L	G	L	E	V	U	M	T
A	U	U	O	O	L	I	N	B	V	T	A	D	A	A
D	M	R	C	R	S	U	R	E	D	O	A	M	G	S
N	C	U	B	A	S	T	R	B	B	C	T	T	U	I
A	A	T	I	T	R	T	E	E	D	E	R	I	S	L
L	L	U	N	N	I	O	O	T	V	T	E	D	S	U
O	C	P	U	L	I	H	B	P	I	U	B	R	E	R
D	A	I	D	E	G	D	P	E	I	M	A	R	I	U
N	R	A	C	S	E	L	N	S	R	T	T	I	U	M
I	I	E	R	U	T	U	C	O	V	E	U	I	U	M
V	A	L	I	V	I	A	R	C	L	N	M	M	U	M

Aquae Sulis	Deva	Londinium
Calcaria	Eboracum	Noviomagus
Calleva Atrebatum	Glevum	Rutupiae
Camulodunum	Lactodorum	Venta Silurum
Corinium	Letocetum	Verulamium
Corstopitum	Lindum	Vindolanda

34   Road numbers

*The object of the puzzle is to find out which letter of the alphabet is represented by each of the 20 numbers used. The missing words are all names of Roman roads in Britain. You are given just one letter to start you off, so you can begin by entering this wherever its number appears in the grid. As you decode each letter, write it in the **Letters deciphered** table and cross it off in the **Letters used** table.*

9	15	6	10	19	8	12							
9	12	1 E		6	15	8	7						
17	10	8	14	1	13	8	10	1					
16	15	17	17	1		19	8	12					
20	8	7	1	17		6	15	8	7				
13	6	1	8	7		6	15	8	7				
7	1	6	1		17	10	6	1	1	10			
2	20	3	14	2	1	4	7		19	8	12		
1	6	5	2	14	1		17	10	6	1	1	10	
8	3	1	5	8	14		17	10	6	1	1	10	
19	8	10	4	2	14	13		17	10	6	1	1	10
7	1	18	2	4	17		11	2	13	11	19	8	12

Letters deciphered

1	2	3	4	5	6	7	8	9	10	11	12	13	14	15	16	17	18	19	20
E																			

Letters used

A	C	D	E̶	F	G	H	I	K	L	M	N	O	P	R	S	T	V	W	Y

35   Buildings all round

Solve this riddle by answering all the statements which follow. As you answer each question, insert a letter in the grid below, where you will see a word formed which was once a Roman building.

1.   My first is apse but never in gateways.
2.   My second is double in turret and fortress.
3.   My third is in Great and also in Bath.
4.   My fourth is in mile and also in castle.
5.   My fifth is in tower and also in rampart.
6.   My sixth is in Old and also in Work.
7.   My seventh is in granary and also horreum.
8.   My eighth does a treble in principia.
9.   My ninth is in tablinum and also in study.
10.   My tenth is mithraeum's top and tail.

The building in question is:

1	2	3	4	5	6	7	8	9	10

To whom was this stone dedicated?

....

What might the purpose of this stone have been?

....

36   Inscriptions IV

See how much you know about abbreviations and letters used in Roman inscriptions. By answering the questions and then inserting the first letters of each answer into the grid below, you should reveal something the inscriptions have in common. In case you don't know much at all about this material, you should refer to the Epigraphy Appendix at the back of this book, which will help you out.

1. This letter was the part of the VSLM formula which meant *for the deserving one.* ....
2. These four letters were used to indicate a cavalryman. ....
3. This letter was used as an abbreviation meaning *soldier.* ....
4. This was the part of the abbreviation IOM which meant *best.* ....
5. This letter was used as an abbreviation to mean *Rufus.* ....
6. This letter was used to mean *first.* ....
7. You might see this three letter abbreviation near the letters *VIX.* ....
8. This letter was the part of the VSLM formula which meant *happily.* ....
9. This four letter word means *for Sulis.* ....

What the inscriptions have in common is:

1	2	3	4	5	6	7	8	9

To which god do you think this stone was dedicated?

....

To what else was it dedicated?

....

Who was the person who made the dedication?

....

DEO·MO
GVNTIE
CEN IOLO
CI
LV PVL
VS VSM

37   Hypocaust sudoku

You know how sudoku works. All you have to do is to place numbers one to nine in each vertical and horizontal line and then make sure that each number appears once in each of the nine 3x3 squares. The difference here is that this is Hypocaust sudoku, named after the Roman central heating system! You have to use the nine letters of this in the same way. Good luck.

P				A		H		Y
	A			P			S	T
Y		T	U	H				
C			P	S			O	U
	U		A		O	T		
	P			H				C
A	Y			O		P		
	S				A	Y		O
T			C	Y		U	A	S

Who dedicated this stone to the old gods?

....

What was the purpose of the stone?

....

38   Wordsearch plus: local produce

There are two parts to this puzzle, which features a set of artefacts found around the country. First off, you should try to match the artefacts on the left with their locations on the right in the lists below.

Antenociticus head	Bath
Birth of Mithras sculpture	Benwell
Bronze head of Minerva	Bignor
Cupid on dolphin mosaic	Carrawburgh
Great silver dish	Corbridge
Lion sculpture	Fishbourne
Mithraic altars	Housesteads
Mosaic of cherub gladiators	Low Ham
Shell mosaic	Mildenhall
Stone statue of Mars	Rudston
Tombstone of Regina	South Shields
Venus mosaic	St Albans
Virgil mosaic	Vindolanda
Writing tablets	York

And now to the grid, where you should find the locations all hidden away. Words may go across, backwards, up, down or diagonally.

S	O	U	T	H	S	H	I	E	L	D	S	C	O	R	I	V	N
U	G	C	B	R	I	D	G	V	U	J	A	N	M	D	V	I	L
F	I	S	H	B	O	U	R	N	E	R	U	D	S	T	O	N	O
B	R	U	D	S	E	Y	O	K	R	V	I	B	T	O	L	D	L
Y	M	I	L	D	E	N	H	A	L	L	A	H	A	H	G	O	N
L	O	W	H	I	G	N	W	J	K	S	D	A	L	T	W	L	L
O	J	R	N	K	Y	B	R	E	F	D	V	P	B	H	H	A	A
B	I	H	K	L	U	L	U	N	L	L	A	H	A	M	N	N	O
F	I	S	H	R	O	N	G	I	B	L	O	M	N	U	R	D	F
R	K	E	G	D	I	R	B	R	O	C	H	E	S	T	E	A	N
U	B	H	J	U	L	S	D	A	E	T	S	E	S	U	O	H	D

39   Out and about in Roman Britain

Test yourself out on your general knowledge of our Romano-British heritage.

Across

7. Street from London to Lincoln (6)
8. Catapult whose name meant *wild ass* (6)
9. Short version of emperor's name (3)
10. What Boudicca did to London (6)
11. Boat driven by slave rowers (6)
12. Original job for a bishop of Constantine (3)
14. A Roman amulet served as one (5)
17. Artistic depiction of beauty or youth (5)
19. Roman gold (5)
20. Body part covered by a lorica (5)
23. Build a Roman camp (5)
26. Thermopolium (3)
28. Hadrian's wife (6)
29. Great Chesters fort (6)
30. First Greek letter of a Christian symbol (3)
31. What happened to coins in London (6)
32. Soldier's pay (6)

Down

1. Petuaria (6)
2. West Sussex villa with cherub gladiator mosaic (6)
3. Cut off and found as skulls in London (5)
4. Damp like Vindolanda earth (5)
5. Protected by Hadrian (6)
6. Lepidina's friend Claudia ...... (6)
13. Roman gateway (5)
15. A Roman hello (3)
16. Made of ferns in Vindolanda (3)
17. Emperor (abbrev.) (3)
18. What you did in the triclinium (3)
21. Prime concern for Bath visitor (6)
22. Writing implement (6)
24. Roman island or apartment block (6)
25. Correspondent of Julius Caesar (6)
26. Protected by shields in a tortoise (5)
27. What a signifer would do with his burden (5)

40 Cryptic Roman Britain

See if you can solve these tricky clues.

Across

7. A cosmic, endless kind of art (6)
8. A foreign sort of treatment for Boudicca (6)
9. Onager's the word for it (3)
10. Complaint heard about import (4)
11. The lady member uses oil (4)
12. Sees past in the bath (3)
13. He will hear about British speciality (3)
14. God of the bar? (4)
16. Hit out at Fishbourne hedge (3)
18. Winsome sounding ledge for wall (4)
20. Tent life in fort (4)
23. Long-standing job at Wroxeter (3)
25. Scrape the top with a strigil (4)
27. Fellow loves Minerva's bird inside (3)
28. Claudius started a Roman one (3)
29. Appear to go first for the plumber (4)
30. Dionysus' toupée, perhaps (4)
31. Numbered Roman niches in Chesters (3)
32. Good health with a pro (6)
33. Officer's glee at confusion (6)

Down

1. Carlo takes one for his chest (6)
2. Embrace scares Venus and Cupid (6)
3. Artist in crust-engraved gem (6)
4. Discover old flame by Bignor (6)
5. Gruesome relics of London outrage (6)
6. Late men took no time for brooch decoration (6)
15. Mithras lost this victim (3)
17. Olive's in the toilet (3)
19. Pen's mate seen on tablet (3)
21. Fake manoeuvres in old road (6)
22. There's quiet hatred for imperial platform (6)
23. Oil producers? So vile! (6)
24. A diabolical highway, maybe (6)
25. Wild barbarian gave as he got (6)
26. Design it eventually around Boudicca's torch (6)

41 Who's in charge?

Complete the grid below by filling in the names of the local rulers and by so doing, reveal a Roman in charge running down the grid.

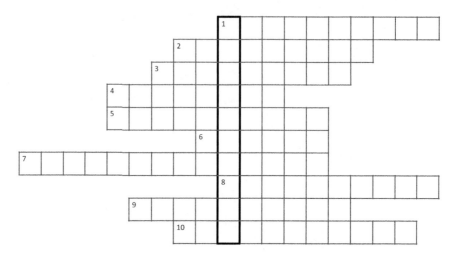

1. This king of the Iceni was once past augurs (10)

2. Act as a cur, like a Catuvellaunian chief (9)

3. Shakespeare's Cymbeline's a cub online (9)

4. A cubic do for revolting queen? (8)

5. Incubus god for Fishbourne king (10)

6. Celtic priests were a dud, Sir (6)

7. An allusive cuss, Caesar's enemy (14)

8. Smug to undo Catuvellaunian king (10)

9. King of the Atrebates omits cumin (7)

10. Aid a curt man for Brigantian queen (11)

The man in charge running down the grid is: ....

42 · Pointing the way

Test yourself out and see if you can fill in the gaps in the table below. All the clues are on the grid.

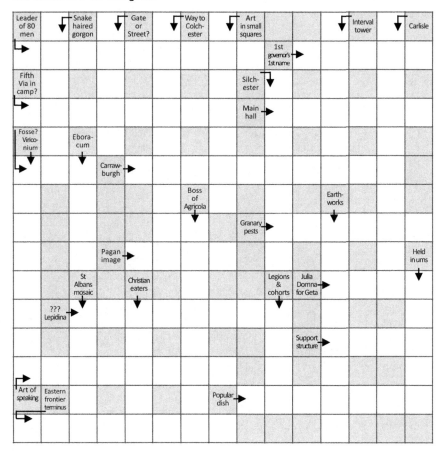

43   Wordsearch: villas in Britain

Roman villas and even a palace have been found around the country. A set of them has been listed below and then hidden in the grid: your job is to find them. Words may go across, backwards, up, down or diagonally.

T	H	R	U	D	S	T	O	N	O	T	X	U	R	H	T
S	H	G	I	E	L	H	T	R	O	N	U	N	N	E	Y
T	R	B	I	G	N	O	R	S	E	L	C	C	E	L	B
O	W	E	L	W	Y	N	N	E	W	P	O	R	T	U	O
N	F	A	R	N	O	T	G	N	I	H	T	I	W	L	X
E	I	D	N	T	H	R	I	N	G	S	I	K	A	L	E
S	S	L	E	S	I	T	H	I	E	I	T	C	D	I	N
F	H	A	R	B	T	H	R	L	U	L	S	O	F	N	R
I	B	M	E	B	R	E	M	O	T	W	E	T	I	G	U
E	O	T	M	E	R	A	A	A	W	A	Y	S	E	S	O
L	U	H	I	B	R	A	D	D	H	D	I	L	L	T	B
D	R	H	T	R	I	N	G	I	G	W	E	A	D	O	K
E	N	T	A	L	O	W	H	A	N	N	O	H	I	N	C
T	E	H	L	U	L	L	I	N	G	G	E	L	C	E	O
S	W	E	G	A	D	E	B	R	I	D	G	E	B	R	R
H	E	M	S	W	M	A	H	G	N	I	T	N	A	R	B

Beadlam	Gadebridge	Rudston
Bignor	Halstock	Stonesfield
Box	Latimer	Thruxton
Brading	Low Ham	Titsey
Brantingham	Lullingstone	Wadfield
Chedworth	Newport	Wanstead
Dawlish	North Leigh	Welwyn
Eccles	Nunney	Wharram le Street
Fishbourne	Rockbourne	Withington

44　An L of a job

Try to fit the words listed below into the grid, all of which have something to do with Roman Britain. Just one letter has been done for you, to get you started.

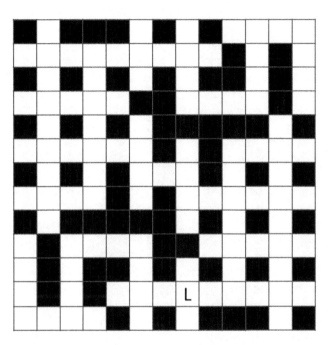

Three letters	Four letters (cont'd)	Six letters
ala	lead	armlet
net	Pict	tavern
via	raid	
	stag	Seven letters
Four letters	turf	
	yoke	Orpheus
apse		rampart
Deva	Five letters	
duty		Nine letters
Eros	carts	
fort	lamps	Caracalla
Gaul		laconicum
ills		milestone
inns		skeletons

45   Help on the wall

There are three parts to this quiz. First, you should identify the answers to each of the first of the pairs of questions below, which you may find a little cryptic. Then, answer the second of each pair of questions with a number. Finally, put the first letters of your first answers in the ascending order of the list of numbers (from low numbers to high) to reveal a group of people who helped the Romans to man Hadrian's Wall.

1.   Governor whose Stanegate frontier system predated the wall (8) ....
How many corner towers were there in a typical fort along the wall? ....

2.   A user lax about three Roman aides (11) ....
What was the original width of the broad wall in Roman feet? ....

3.   Sun god takes path to western wall's end ....
Approximately how many men were stationed at Housesteads fort? ....

4.   Avian King of Northumberland makes fort on the line (9) ....
How many turrets were built between each milecastle on the wall? ....

5.   Right in river by Willowford and Brampton (7) ....
What was the age of Emperor Hadrian when he first came to Northumberland? ....

6.   No coals for this Aelian Bridge (9,4,4) ....
In what year AD did the building of the wall start? ....

7.   Loveless torture confused lookout on the wall (6) ....
How many gates were there at Chesters fort? ....

8.   Group of three in Carrawburgh Mithraeum heard changes (6) ....
What is the length of the wall in miles? ....

9.   Rival lumberjacks surround southside system (6) | ....
To the nearest round number, how many men might be stationed in a milecastle? ....

Some people who helped to man the wall were:

46 Inscriptions V

See how much you know about abbreviations and letters used in Roman inscriptions. By answering the questions and then inserting the first letters of each answer into the grid below, you should reveal something the inscriptions have in common. In case you don't know much at all about this material, you should refer to the Epigraphy Appendix at the back of this book, which will help you out.

1. This is the word which means *discharged* in a four letter gravestone formula which means "discharged the vow happily for the deserving one". ....

2. These two letters were used to mean *second*. ....

3. These three letters were used to mean a *legion*. ....

4. This two letter word might precede *testamento*, meaning something had been performed according to the instructions of a will. ....

5. This letter stood for the Latin word meaning *most noble*. ....

6. This letter was used as an abbreviation for the name *Titus*. ....

7. This letter was used as an abbreviation to mean a *vow* or an *offering*. ....

8. This letter was used as an abbreviation to mean *the best*. ....

9. This letter was used as an abbreviation to mean *for Jupiter*. ....

10. These three letters were used to refer to a *consul*. ....

11. This two letter word meant *and*. ....

12. This letter is the part of the formula *HSE* which means *buried*. ....

What the inscriptions have in common is:

1	2	3	4	5	6	7	8	9	10	11	12

To whom was this stone dedicated?

....

Exactly how old was this person?

....

What was the purpose of this inscription and how do we know?

....

You know how sudoku works. All you have to do is to place numbers one to nine in each vertical and horizontal line and then make sure that each number appears once in each of the nine 3x3 squares. The difference here is that this is Cold baths sudoku, so-called after a rather disturbing habit the Romans had when finishing off their visits to the thermae. You have to use the nine letters of this phrase in the same way. Good luck.

S		C		D	B		A	H
				H	O	T		
H	A		O		C			S
O						B		
D		B	L	S		T		O
	L		B				H	D
	S		A		D	H	L	
		L	H	B		C		T
B			C	O				A

This stone was dedicated to the mothers - but what or who do you think these mothers might have been?

....

To what else was this stone dedicated?

....

48   Wordsearch plus: galleries galore

There are two parts to this puzzle, which features a set of museums with interesting Roman collections. First off, you should try to match the museums on the left with their locations on the right in the lists below.

Ashmolean Museum	Bath
British Museum	Caerleon
Corinium Museum	Cambridge
Fitzwilliam Museum	Carvoran
Great North Museum	Chester
Grosvenor Museum	Cirencester
Hunterian Museum	Glasgow
National Roman Legion	London
Roman Army Museum	Newcastle
Roman Baths Museum	Oxford
The Undercroft Museum	St Albans
Verulamium Museum	York

And now to the grid, where you should find the locations all hidden away. Words may go across, backwards, up, down or diagonally.

C	Y	O	X	K	N	H	R	E	T	S	E	H	C
C	I	X	K	O	R	B	R	O	K	L	K	B	L
A	E	R	O	X	F	O	R	D	T	F	R	O	D
R	G	S	E	S	T	A	Y	S	Y	N	N	K	B
V	D	T	B	N	E	E	A	X	O	D	H	L	G
O	I	A	A	D	C	C	R	E	O	L	T	L	L
R	R	L	T	O	W	E	L	N	U	F	A	B	N
A	B	B	E	E	K	R	S	B	B	S	Y	R	T
N	M	A	N	Y	E	N	M	T	G	R	E	A	G
O	A	N	B	A	T	H	J	O	E	B	R	Y	N
F	C	S	C	A	M	B	W	R	O	R	X	T	E

49   All about Roman Britain

The clues are as confused as can be and your answers should be relevant somehow! Good luck with this one.

Across

8. Spurious coastal changes for the second Roman governor (8,7)
9. Enemy attack (4)
10. Pungent fish sauce (5)
11. It's home to the Grosvenor Museum (4)
12. Where the Pharos once lit things up (6)
14. Governor Philippus first came out in unison (6)
16. A short emperor (3)
18. Boudicca's one from the Eastern part (7)
19. Takes off from pointless scene of Christian crime (7)
20. Snare for trident man (3)
22. State of readiness in camp (2,4)
24. Be certain there'll not be a local revolt (6)
25. Sarcophagus, perhaps (4)
27. Legionaries' bird (5)
28. Original amphora? (4)
29. Fed noxious cider, confused and damned by lead tablet (6,2,7)

Down

1. If upset, do mourn musician at the end of the Fosse Way (4,11)
2. Celtic war paint (4)
3. Conflicts of the Maiden Castle variety (6)
4. Brigantian fort near Boroughbridge (7)
5. Military awareness like Agricola's (6)
6. How Suetonius Paulinus moved from Mona to London (4)
7. Reclusive if alas confused prefect of Batavians at Vindolanda (7,8)
13. Straight line for an emperor (5)
15. Granaries in forts provided for basic ones (5)
16. Mansio (3)
17. Common container (3)
21. Get lean for refined art trip (7)
23. They gave rides around Chesters fort (6)
24. Tribal capital in Devon (6)
26. Portrait seems broken (4)
28. It's a valuable place for an emperor's head (4)

50   Grand old Roman Britain

Test out your knowledge on pretty much anything related.

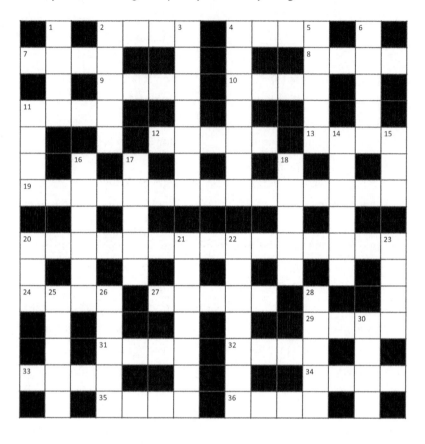

Across

2. Space for cubiculum? (4)
4. Altar stone toupé for a sun god, perhaps (4)
7. Peacock goddess (4)
8. Roof or box - it's the same stuff (4)
9. Legion, cohort or century (4)
10. She put Narcissus on repeat (4)
11. Ox-driven transport (4)
12. Cornucopia filling (5)
13. It provided Jupiter's hold on Ganymede (4)
19. It's at the western end of Hadrian's wall (7,2,6)
20. Collection of military material at Carvoran (5,4,6)
24. Inspirational goddess (4)
27. Focus on dedication stone (5)
29. Location for an iron age fort (4)
31. Each upset's a reason to go to Bath (4)
32. Actor boss who saw off rebellion (4)
33. Hadrian's limits across the Empire (4)
34. Direction to Iceni home (4)
35. Corny parts of tauroctony display (4)
36. Makes hole in excavations (4)

Down

1. A Roman moon (4)
2. Via out in about (5)
3. God of light and truth found in London and Carrawburgh (7)
4. Retain a bewildered German auxiliary (7)
5. Careful thinker in a porch (5)
6. Goddess in full bloom (5)
11. Grooming accessory made of wood or bone (4)
14. Prime mover in the Basilica (6)
15. Travel via Fosse or Icknield (3)
16. Places of escape for Celts during the early occupation (6)
17. Plants used for matting in the Vindolanda vicus (5)
18. Meeting in the marketplace (5)
20. Horny and battered by breaking and entering (3)
21. Carvings projected from a flat surface (7)
22. What Auden's soldier did while suffering the blues (7)
23. Bardon grinder locates Chesterholm museum (4)
25. Cleansing waste product taxed by Vespasian (5)
26. A seer can deal with Geta, damn him! (5)
28. Caligae (5)
30. It's Cupid's thing (4)

51   Buried in museums

All sorts of wonderful things can be found in our Romano-British museums. Complete the table by answering the clues and by so doing, discover a concealed artefact running down the grid.

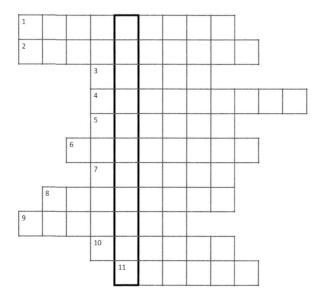

1.   Let some in to mark the way (9)
2.   Red pottery found in a warm sea (6,4)
3.   Instrument seen in long romance (5)
4.   Statues from pure cults (9)
5.   Change car oil for protection (6)
6.   Keep safe in ham opera (8)
7.   Choir takes an hour for iconic display (3,3)
8.   Common coin's as ruined as could be (8)
9.   Girls take it about for scraping skin (7)
10.   Pursue a former golden oldie but don't keep quiet (6)
11.   Lust is what you need to make your mark (6)

The concealed artefact is a: ....

52   Fragments sudoku

You know how sudoku works. All you have to do is to place numbers one to nine in each vertical and horizontal line and then make sure that each number appears once in each of the nine 3x3 squares. The difference here is that this is Fragments sudoku, so-called after all the bits and pieces we find and interpret across Roman Britain. You have to use the nine letters of this word in the same way. Good luck.

N		A		E		F	R	
S		R			G	E		M
	T		F	A			N	G
R		N	M			T		A
			R		A			E
A		G	T		N	M		R
G			E	N			T	S
E		T	A			G		F
	R	S		M				N

This was a marker stone for a particular group of soldiers. What can you say about them?   ....

The two mythical animals seen here were both associated with the second legion. Can you name them?   ....
....

53   Double trouble - battering Celts

Put your answers to the clues in the grids below. You may have one problem, however: there are two questions for each of the clues and you have to decide into which grid the right answers should go. Two words have been given to start you off. Good luck.

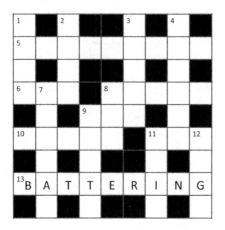

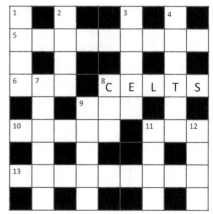

Across

5. Camp headquarters (9) *** The study of inscriptions (9)
6. One thing you'd expect to see on a gravestone (3) *** Mithras was ... invictus (3)
8. Local tribespeople (5) *** Son of Venus (5)
9. Thermopolium (3) *** Jupiter the greatest and the best (Abbrev.) (1,1,1)
10. Litters (5) *** Something to do in the cubiculum (5)
11. Mosaics and paintings (3) *** Weapon of a retiarius (3)
13. Ram's action (9) *** State in which to leave the apodyterium on the way to the caldarium (9)

Down

1. Chester (4) *** A building style, eg .... *reticulatum* (4)
2. A Roman drink (4) *** Common site to find a fort (4)
3. Body part scanned by a haruspex (5) *** Doncaster (5)
4. Bodyguard of a leading official (6) *** Religious monument (6)
7. Shape of a Roman fort (6) *** Modern version of a cithara (6)
8. Consul (Abbrev.) (3) *** Garment worn by Mercury (3)
9. Hadrian's facial hair (5) *** How Romans left Boudicca feeling (5)
11. Iron fixing (4) *** Round alcove (4)
12. Woollen garment (4) *** Coastal surge which took Caesar by surprise (4)

54　Notes by numbers

The object of the puzzle is to find out which letter of the alphabet is represented by each of the 21 numbers used. The missing words are all connected with archaeology in Roman Britain. You are given just one letter to start you off, so you can begin by entering this wherever its number appears in the grid. As you decode each letter, write it in the **Letters deciphered** *table and cross it off in the* **Letters used** *table.*

5	18	7	21	4									
3	19	4	1	12	10								
3	19	2	11	4	6								
18	19	2	17	9	6	4							
12	10	19	2	1	2	6	2	15	16				
4	20	12	7	8	7	3	9	2	1				
12	19	2	5	5	21	7	3	9	1	15			
17	9	4	6	21		1 **N**	2 **O**	3 **T**	4 **E**	5 **S**			
12	2	1	5	4	19	8	7	3	9	2	1		
13	7	15	1	4	3	2	13	4	3	19	16		
5	3	19	7	3	9	15	19	7	18	10	16		
5	14	19	17	7	12	4		5	14	19	8	4	16

Letters deciphered

1	2	3	4	5	6	7	8	9	10	11	12	13	14	15	16	17	18	19	20	21
N	O	T	E	S																

Letters used

A	C	D	E̶	F	G	H	I	L	M	N̶	O̶	P	R	S̶	T̶	U	V	W	X	Y

55 View from Rome: the thick of it

The Roman view of Britain was not always positive. As you fill in the grid below, some boxes are numbered and where you see these numbers appear elsewhere on this page, they always represent the same letters. Your final job is to reveal a Roman opinion of Britain in the table below.

1	3		3	12	11	13	2	21		13
3	1	15	17		12	5	4	19	15	1
5	10	8	7	18	5	6	8	15	12	
7	18	18	2	17	8	16	11	5		
9	21	3	13	23	10	6	1	10	11	
11	13	1	15	12	12	12	21	12	18	
13	11	1	1	18	14	16	23	17		
15	11	20	10	1	10	5	16	6	10	21
17	19	11	12	23	14	13	18	16	1	

1. Wild-sounding enemies (10)
2. The Roman god of war (4)
3. Member of an elite Roman fighting force (9)
4. Bird seen as a symbol on a Roman standard (5)
5. Footsoldiers (8)
6. This catapult had a name which originally meant *wild ass* (6)
7. Roman tortoise formation (7)
8. Fighters on horseback (7)
9. Unexpected attack (6)
10. Set of posts set up as a defensive wall (8)

11. Soldier who fired weapons through the air (7)
12. A bank of earth raised up as a defence (7)
13. A type of catapult (8)
14. Roman unit of around 500 men (6)
15. Non-citizen Roman fighter (9)
16 Roman javelin designed to buckle on impact (5)
17. Fortifications made from large scale soil-shifting (10)
18. British tribal warrior (4)

	18	23	19		11	14	7	20	1		1	10	18	18	1	19	
3	12	10	18	13		16	11	8	8	17	18		18	23	12	17	14
13	6	19	11	12	13		14	23	19	8		12	10	2	10	8	15

56   Inscriptions VI

See how much you know about abbreviations and letters used in Roman inscriptions. By answering the questions and then inserting the first letters of each answer into the grid below, you should reveal something the inscriptions have in common. In case you don't know much at all about this material, you should refer to the Epigraphy Appendix at the back of this book, which will help you out.

1. This letter stands for the word which means *Master*.   ....
2. This letter represents the Latin word meaning *is*.   ....
3. This letter stands for the word which means *days*.   ....
4. This letter is the first one in the set of three referring to Jupiter the best and the greatest.   ....
5. This letter stands for the number one hundred and is also used to mean a century (which rather confusingly meant about 80 men).   ....
6. This letter was used as an abbreviation for the name *Aulus*.   ....
7. This letter was used as an abbreviation for the name *Titus*.   ....
8. This letter was used to represent the number one or to mean *the first*.   ....
9. This letter is the second one in the set of three referring to Jupiter the best and the greatest.   ....
10. This letter was used to mean *our*.   ....
11. This word meant *the Senate*.   ....

What the inscriptions have in common is:

1	2	3	4	5	6	7	8	9	10	11
										.

This fragmentary inscription seems to name a Roman emperor on the first line. Can you identify him?

....

Another famous person seems to appear on the second line. Can you guess whose name this may be?

....

57   Drill exercise

See if you can fit the words listed into the grid below. One word has been done for you, to get you started.

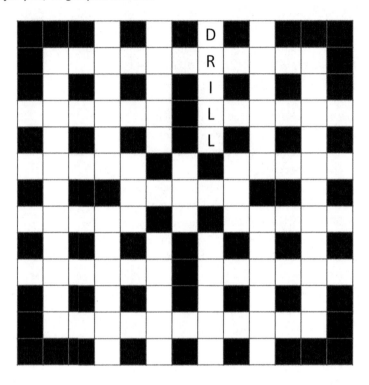

Three letters	Five letters	Six letters	Eleven letters
axe	angle	Druids	Chesterholm
era	~~drill~~	gorgon	Corstopitum
ode	envoy	legate	metalworker
	metal	legion	multangular
	opera	neatly	
	radix	rebels	
	stage	stable	
	stash	tracks	
	stone		

58   Double trouble - Stonegate rebellion

Put your answers to the clues in the grids below. You may have one problem, however: there are two questions for each of the clues and you have to decide into which grid the right answers should go. Two words have been given to start you off. Good luck.

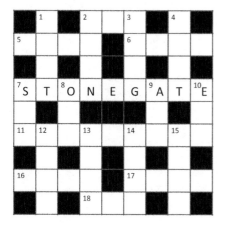

Across

2. Nervous trait of Claudius (3) *** Excavate (3)
5. Emperor in whose reign Boudicaa revolted (4) *** Roman game (4)
6. Entrance to a mine derived from Latin word meaning *approaches* (4) *** Via (4)
7. ~~Boudiccan revolt (9)~~ *** ~~Street in York where via praetoria once ran (9)~~
11. May have described some visitors to Roman Bath (9) *** Writing equipment (3,6)
16. Hadrian's Wall milecastle, Harrows …. (4) *** Animal for arena (4)
17. Material used for wall-building in rapid construction projects (4) *** Beasts with pulling power (4)
18. Cohort (Abbrev.) (3) *** X (3)

Down

1. In the inscription *IOM*, it's what *O* means (4) *** 1000 paces (4)
2. Municipium (4) *** Road leading North from York, …. Street (4)
3. France (4) *** Lake below Hadrian's Wall …. Lough (4)
4. Condiment paid to soldiers (4) *** Lover of Aeneas in Low Ham mosaic (4)
7. Bath (3) *** What slaves did in galleys (3)
8. Hedging tree (3) *** Centurion's number 2 (Abbrev.) (3)
9. How you'd feel in a *valetudinarium* (3) *** What you'd do on a *scaena* (3)
10. And a hundred (Abbrev.) (3) *** Fruit of a tree called *nux* in Latin (3)
12. Support structure (4) *** Dilapidated building (4)
13. Celtic necklace (4) *** Pastime of Emperor Hadrian (4)
14. Cold or hot restoration (4) *** Commonly used metal (4)
15. A bad March day for Julius Caesar (4) *** What Mark Antony wanted to borrow after that day (4)

59 Wordsearch plus: filling faces

There are two parts to this puzzle, which features a set of foodstuffs and drinks consumed in Roman Britain. First off, you should try to match the items on the left with their Latin names on the right in the lists below.

beer	acetum
bread	cervisia
chicken	condimenta
eggs	lardum
honey	mel
oil	oleum
olives	olivae
oysters	ostreae
pepper	ova
pig fat	panis
radishes	piper
salt	pullus
spices	radices
vinegar	sal
wine	vinum

And now to the grid, where you should find the locations all hidden away. Words may go across, backwards, up, down or diagonally.

A	E	A	E	R	T	S	O	M	A	O	C	M	A
T	E	V	R	L	S	E	V	L	R	V	S	E	R
N	A	C	C	E	R	V	I	S	I	A	M	C	A
E	S	M	A	M	E	M	U	N	I	V	S	S	D
M	R	U	A	C	N	C	R	M	V	C	A	O	I
I	V	D	L	E	E	S	N	I	U	S	L	E	C
D	M	R	R	L	I	T	P	I	P	E	R	V	E
N	C	A	A	N	U	I	U	N	U	R	E	M	S
O	C	L	A	S	S	P	U	M	C	S	V	C	A
C	E	P	V	A	M	C	R	U	E	M	N	U	S
A	E	A	E	R	T	S	O	R	A	O	R	M	V

60   View from Rome: a rough bunch

The Roman view of Britain was not always positive. As you fill in the grid below, some boxes are numbered and where you see these numbers appear elsewhere on this page, they always represent the same letters. Your final job is to reveal a Roman opinion of Britain in the table below.

1	5		4	22	13	14			5		2	19		8
3	11		20	21			17		3	4			17	10
5		1	1	6	19		17	6	21	12		20		
7	6		18	16	4			8	1		17	6		
9	2		6		23	10	23		8	11	23	19		16
12	8	3		3		13	6	20	3					23
14		8	13		15	1	13	22			4		9	
16	14	23	1	9	17	21		17			19	12		16
18	18		22	19	6			23		12	5	4		3

1. Tribal folk from the Suffolk and Essex area (11)
2. Material used in tablets for writing (3)
3. Site of a Roman palace near Chichester (10)
4. Eboracum (4)
5. Campaign described in an account by Julius Caesar (6,3)
6. Hot or cold, you find them all around the country (5)
7. Invading emperor (8)
8. Latin word for a breastplate (6)
9. Northern tribesfolk (5)
10. VI (3)
11. Gladius (5)
12. Isca Dumnoniorum (6)
13. Cavalry fort on Hadrian's Wall (8)
14. Name given to a shore fort such as Pevensey (5)
15. Latin name for London (9)
16 Inscription meaning *discharged the vow happily for the deserving one* (1,1,1,1)
17. Fort near Greenhead on Hadrian's Wall (10)
18. Container for ashes (3)
19. Great emperor at York (11)

3	8	2	3	6	5	■	22	13	22	3	■	13	11	■	5	20	3	9
■	5	13	■	21	3	■	23	10	4	1	1	3	16	■	4	22	■	■
9	18	23	4	6	■	13	17	■	1	4	5	3	17	12	5	18	17	3

61 Construction projects

Complete the table below by filling in your answers and by so doing, discover a concealed construction running down the grid.

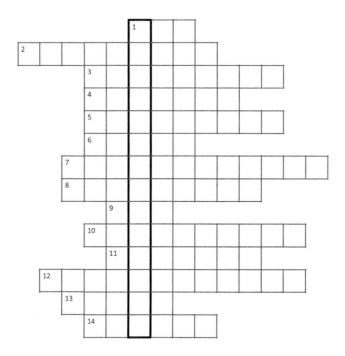

1. You'll find your way in the aviary (3)
2. Mum takes in the air in place of initiation (9)
3. Can noodle about along covered porchway (9)
4. Confused there, at place of entertainment (7)
5. He has bout of chaos when he goes for a wash here (4,5)
6. Cut or run to the basilica (5)
7. Principia's top of all four (12)
8. Stranger takes tipsy leer at ornate garden (9)
9. Beginner's inside the mansio (3)
10. Take auto primer to commander's house (10)
11. Short elderly relative confused Ray in the barn (7)
12. Met the pariah here for the show (12)
13. There's no stand for umpire in the market (5)
14. Lame pet is missing a sanctuary (6)

The concealed site is: ....

62 Discovery sudoku

You know how sudoku works. All you have to do is to place numbers one to nine in each vertical and horizontal line and then make sure that each number appears once in each of the nine 3x3 squares. The difference here is that this is Discovery sudoku, so-called after our various voyages around Roman Britain. You have to use the nine letters of this word in the same way. Good luck.

	O	V		E		Y		
	Y			D		E		
C			Y	V			I	
R			C	Y	E			V
	C						S	
V		O		S	I	C		R
	V			I	Y		D	
	I	D		R		O	C	
		S		C			E	

Which god is shown on this stone?

....

What is the figure doing at the bottom on the left?

....

....

63 Double trouble - Birley in urns

Put your answers to the clues in the grids below. You may have one problem, however: there are two questions for each of the clues and you have to decide into which grid the right answers should go. Two words have been given to start you off. Good luck.

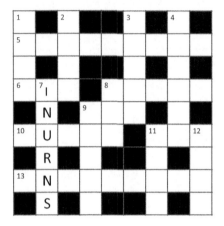

Across

5. Scotland (9) *** Hot room (9)
6. Tiberius (Abbrev.) (3) *** Latin eggs (3)
8. Country house (5) *** Inner chamber of a temple (5)
9. Soft metal mined in Cornwall (3) *** Jupiter or Neptune (3)
10. Battering or Zodiac ram (5) *** Shellfish valuable for its purple dye (5)
11. Symbol for the world held in Jupiter's hand (3) *** ... Road, running from Norwich to Colchester (3)
13. Kills one in ten (9) *** Valetudinarium (9)

Down

1. A modern day Pict (4) *** Nymph beloved of Narcissus (4)
2. Weapon held by Hercules (4) *** Pot for cooking or storage (4)
3. Togate (5) *** Sewer (5)
4. Archaeologist family of Vindolanda (6) *** Launderer (6)
7. Writings of Virgil or Horace (6) *** Where you might keep the ashes of the dead (2,4)
8. Consul (Abbrev.) (3) *** Lived (Abbrev.) (3)
9. Temperature of a warm room (5) *** For the spirit (epigraphy) (5)
11. Gemstone (4) *** Storage vessels (4)
12. Ones who put on the manly toga (4) *** Direction from where Mithras and Isis came (4)

64 Digging in the dirt

*The object of the puzzle is to find out which letter of the alphabet is represented by each of the 21 numbers used. The missing words are all people who have served archaeology in Roman Britain. You are given just one name to start you off, so you can begin by entering the letters of this wherever their numbers appear elsewhere in the grid. As you decode each letter, write it in the **Letters deciphered** table and cross it off in the **Letters used** table.*

21	2	19	16		8	15	17	9	14										
1	8	15	2	4		1	3	9	10	14									
3	9	1	2	14		B (1)	I (2)	R (3)	L (4)	E (5)	Y (6)								
11	9	13	14		19	4	8	6	17	9	14								
18	13	2	4		13	8	3	12	2	14	7								
18	5	17	5	3		15	8	4	10	8	6								
18	5	17	5	3		8	12	12	6	21	8	14							
17	9	14	6		3	9	1	2	14	15	9	14							
15	13	5	18	18	8	3	12		20	3	5	3	5						
17	2	21	9	17	13	6		18	9	17	17	5	3						
21	9	3	17	2	21	5	3		10	13	5	5	4	5	3				
4	2	14	12	15	8	6		8	4	4	8	15	9	14	11	9	14	5	15

Letters deciphered

1	2	3	4	5	6	7	8	9	10	11	12	13	14	15	16	17	18	19	20	21
B	I	R	L	E	Y															

Letters used

A	B̶	C	D	E̶	F	G	H	I̶	J	K	L̶	M	N	O	P	R̶	S	T	W	Y̶

65   View from Rome: a poor outlook

The Roman view of Britain was not always positive. As you fill in the grid below, some boxes are numbered and where you see these numbers appear elsewhere on this page, they always represent the same letters. Your final job is to reveal a Roman opinion of Britain in the table below.

1	2		12	12	20		15	11				2	12	2	
3		4	18		4	1		15		23	4		5		23
5	2	8	12	21	9				13	6	21		18		
7	23	13	8		11			23	8	10		15		4	
9	18		14	17		10		10	8	11	20	14			20
12		20	19	21			13	8		15	10		23		7
14	8	22		8		15	2	7	5		14				13
16	11			1	17	14			14	2	3			3	
18	12		1	19	16	12		15	20			12		17	1

1.   Zig-zag pattern of tiles (11)
2.   Greek letter often seen with Chi (3)
3.   Latin name for Chichester (10)
4.   Generic name for a building style (4)
5.   Roman Fort on a Cumbrian hilltop (9)
6.   Site of a lighthouse overlooking the Channel (5)
7.   Verulamium (2,6)
8.   Unit of around 5000 soldiers (6)
9.   Civilian settlement (5)
10. Wing of cavalry (3)
11. Boudicca's tribe (5)
12. Latin name for Lincoln (6)
13. Druid island (8)
14. Latin waters of Bath (5)
15. Underfloor heating system (9)
16   Flat side of Vallum (4)
17. Camulodunum (10)
18. Animal used for battering (3)
19. Cold room at the baths (11)

13	2	3		23	9	7		20	23		15	2	8	23	13	10	7
6	20	13	2		16	12	3	22	17	3	19	13		12	8	20	19
23	2	4	6	3	12	23		8	19	21		14	10	4	17	21	23

Solutions

1 Around and about in Roman Britain

```
D O V E R
  B I G N O R
  L I N C O L N
L O N D O N
  G L O U C E S T E R
  S I L C H E S T E R
    B A T H
C I R E N C E S T E R
  C H E D W O R T H
      C A E R L E O N
```

The answer: VINDOLANDA
Here you can view remarkable remains of Roman writing tablets, leatherwear and a pre-Hadrianic fort.

2 Hadrian's Wall sites

```
  C H E S T E R S
  A       H           C
A R B E I A   L O O S   V
  V       E         R   I
  O       L   B R U N T O N
  R       D   E       E   D
W A L L S E N D     R   O
  N     O       W   M   V   L
        U     A E S I C A   A
C R A G     G   L   T   L   N
  I     H       L   H   L   D
  G             R   U   A
    G A T E S       A   M
                    S
```

The answer: CORBRIDGE

3 Wordsearch: British tribes

4 X marks the spot

```
H A R D K N O T T P A S S
      I       U   A     O
  I   D R A I N A G E   L
  C   I       I   A     D
M E D U S A   C A N T I I
  N   S   X       S     E
O I L   C E R E S   W A R
  L   E       G   C   Q
I N S U L A   G A L L U S
C     R   U       I     A
A   B O U L O G N E   E
N     P   U       N
A L T A R S O F S T O N E
```

5 Issues of occupation

1. Anglesey, 300 miles
2. Agricola, 6 or 7 (it's a bit unclear)
3. Eagles, 1
4. St Albans, 80,000
5. Exeter, AD 47
6. Trinovantes, 400
7. Temple, 4 legions
8. Gallic, 8 years
9. Nero, AD 60

The answer: STANEGATE
This frontier system was left to secure the North of the province after Agricola's recall to Rome.

6 Inscriptions I

1. COH (cohors)
2. ANN (annos)
3. R
4. VIX (vixit)
5. E (est)
6. D (dies)
7. I (Iovi)
8. NUM (numini)
9. S (situs)
10. T
11. OPT (optio)
12. NA (natus, nata)
13. ET

The answer: CARVED IN STONE
The stone (RIB 1709) tells us that Celer was from the century of the leading centurion.

7 Brigantes sudoku

```
A S R  I E G  B T N
E N T  S A B  G I R
G B I  R T N  A E S
I G E  T R A  N S B
T R N  B I S  E A G
B A S  N G E  T R I
S E A  G B I  R N T
R I G  A N T  S B E
N T B  E S R  I G A
```

Julius Primus was the centurion in charge. The inscription (RIB 1711) is very difficult to read.

Bath	Aquae Sulis
Carlisle	Luguvalium
Chester	Deva
Cirencester	Corinium
Colchester	Camulodunum
Dover	Dubris
Exeter	Isca Dumnoniorum
Gloucester	Glevum
Lincoln	Lindum
London	Londinium
Silchester	Calleva Atrebatum
South Shields	Arbeia
St Albans	Verulamium
York	Eboracum

T	H	E	A	T	R	E	S				
					R	O	A	D	S		
					A	M	P	H	O	R	A	E
				M	O	S	A	I	C	S	
W	A	L	L	L	P	A	I	N	T	I	N	G	S
					V	I	L	L	A	S	
	M	I	L	E	S	T	O	N	E	S	
					B	A	T	H	S		
				S	T	A	T	U	E	S	
E	D	U	C	A	T	I	O	N			
				H	Y	P	O	C	A	U	S	T	S
				W	I	N	E				

The answer: ROMANISATION
This was the process of making life more appealing to the British, so they would happily accept Roman rule.

9   Out and about in Roman Britain

(grid puzzle)

L	M	U	R	O	I	N	O	N	M	U	D	A	C	S	I
U	E	D	E	V	A			G	L	E	V	U	M		S
G		B			Q										I
U			O	C	A	M	U	L	O	D	U	N	U	M	R
V			R			A	I	E	B	R	A				B
C	A	L	L	E	V	A	A	T	R	E	B	A	T	U	M	U
L					C			S							D
I					U			M	U	D	N	I	L	
M	U	I	N	I	R	O	C		M			L		
	M			V	E	R	U	L	A	M	I	U	M	I
	M	U	I	N	I	D	N	O	L					S

12   Romano-British roads

W	A	T	L	I	N	G	S	T	R	E	E	T
	K											
D	E	R	E	S	T	R	E	E	T	M	O	O	R
	M		T			R				I		
V	I	A		A		M				L		
	N			N		I	C	K	N	I	E	L	D
	E					N				T		
	G					E	S	T	A	N	E	
P	O	R	T	W	A	Y				R		
		T								Y		
F	O	S	S	E	W	A	Y					

The answer: PAVEMENT
This is the name given to the surface of a Roman road.

13   Wordsearch: Roman Britons

	C				B	O	U	D	I	C	C	A		
	A	A					S				A			
	L		S			U				R			N	
P	B	C	U	S		N				A			I	
R	A	A	N	U	I	A				T			L	
A	N	L	M	N		V	V			A			E	
S		G	U	B		O	E			C			B	C
U		A	D	U		I	N	L		U			O	
T		C	O	D		C	U		L	S		M	N	
A		U	G	I		S	T			A	M		U	
G		S	O	G		A	I			I	U		C	
U			T	O		T	U		U			N		
S				C			S	S					U	
C	A	R	T	I	M	A	N	D	U	A				S
S	U	I	M	M	O	C	N	I	T					
			D	R	U	I	D	S						

9   Out and about in Roman Britain

	P		S		I		G		D	
C	E	L	T	I	C		A	X	E	S
	R		A		K	I	T		V	
W	I	C	K		N		E	R	A	S
	S		E		I		H			
C	H	E	S	T	E	R	H	O	L	M
		A			L		O		E	
G	E	T	A		D	O	R	S	E	T
	R		P	A	W		S		W	
P	O	T	S		A	K	E	M	A	N
	S		E		Y		S		Y	

10   Cryptic Roman Britain

L	I	G	H	T		D	O	V	E	R
A		R		E	G	O		A		I
T	R	A	I	N		M	O	U	N	D
I			T	I	N		L		E	
N	I	N	T	H		A	L	T	A	R
	N		I			E		V		
E	N	A	C	T		A	G	G	E	R
A		U		E	A	R		E		U
G	A	R	U	M		M	E	N	A	I
L		E		P	Y	E		I		N
E	V	I	C	T		D	R	I	P	S

14   Numbers on the wall

```
F O R T
D I T C H
V A L L U M
T U R R E T
G R A N A R Y
G A T E W A Y
L A T R I N E S
B A R R A C K S
P R I N C I P I A
M I L E C A S T L E
P R A E T O R I U M
M I L I T A R Y   R O A D
```

15   A work of art

```
S H E L L M O S A I C
```

The answer: SHELL MOSAIC
This beautiful artefact can be seen in Verulamium Museum. The stone (RIB 1684) was dedicated to Fortune of the Roman People by Gaius (or Caius) Julius from Raetia (Germany) who served in the Victorious Sixth Legion.

16   Inscriptions II

1.   M (menses)
2.   AUG
3.   DM (dis manibus)
4.   EX
5.   TIB
6.   O (optimo)
7.   LEG
8.   A
9.   S
10. TRIB (tribunus)

The answer: MADE TO LAST
The stone (RIB 1708) was placed by soldiers from the 20th legion Valeria Victrix, which is mentioned here. The boar was its mascot or emblem.

17   Legionary sudoku

```
L G E I R O N A Y
R A I E N Y L O G
Y O N A G L E R I
A I R Y O E G L N
G N L R A I O Y E
O E Y N L G R I A
E Y O G I R A N L
I L A O E N Y G R
N R G L Y A I E O
```

This stone (RIB 3345) is a fragment of a dedication, probably an offering.

18   Wordsearch plus: where's that?

Amphitheatre	Chester
Civilian vicus	Vindolanda
Fort reconstruction	South Shields
Great Bath	Bath
Latrine block	Housesteads
Legionary barracks	Caerleon
Lighthouse	Dover
Military bath house	Chesters
Mithraeum	London
Multangular tower	York
Old Work	Wroxeter
Palace	Fishbourne
Temple of Claudius	Colchester
Theatre	St Albans

```
V I N D O L A N D A B           F
N C D Y       A             I
O O H O U S E S T E A D S     S
E L R V N w H   C           H
L C K   E O R H             B
R H       R D E O           O
E E         S N   X         U
A S       T     O   E       R
C T     E S N A B L A T S   N
C H E S T E R S           E E
  R S D L E I H S H T U O S R
```

19   Out and about in Roman Britain

```
  E   P       S   I
R A T A E   B L O C K
  G   G       A   E
A L B A N   S T O N E
  E   N I C H E   I
      N   O
  P   S T E E D   F
F I R T H   S A X O N
  L   A       N   C
R U I N S   A U G U R
  M   E       M   S
```

20   Cryptic Roman Britain

```
  M   K   M   C   S
A U X I L I A R I E S
  L   N   L   A   T
S T A G   E I G H T Y
  A       C       L
U N E X C A V A T E D
  G       S       M
T U R R E T   O V E N
  L   A   L   X   N
B A T T L E M E N T S
  R   S   S   N   S
```

71

The answer: MATRONAE
This was a name for ladies in Roman times.

22   Taking directions

```
   G    F        A   B   W       I
D  R  U  I  D  S     T  O  R  T  O  I  S  E
   A     S     I     R     I     M     C
A  M  P  H  I  T  H  E  A  T  R  E     A
   P     B     E     B     A     N  U  D  E
W  I  D  O  W     P  A  I  N  T        U
   A     U              T     N     G     M
E  N  T  R  A  N  C  E     I     L  U  N  T
   S     N     E     S  L  A  V  E     O
V     C  E  L  T  S     E           V     N
I     A        E  G  G     T  U  N  I  C
C     E     P     V     I        M     O
U     S  H  O  R  E  F  O  R  T     U  R  N
S  P  A     R     R     N           U
      R  I  T  U  A  L  S     G  R  O  M  A
```

23   Wordsearch: the occupation

```
E        C  O  G  I  D  U  B  N  U  S     R
M  A  S  N  A  B  L  A  T  S        E
P     U        R  O  C  H  E  S  T  E  R
E  S  C  L  O  N  D  O  N        S  O  H
R  E  A     U              E     G     G
O  T  T        S        H        O  A  U
R  N  A           P     C        D  T  O
C  A  R           L              U  R  R
L  V  A        I  O     A        M  E  O
A  O  C     A  C  C  I  D  U  O  B  N  B  B
U  N        E           V  T     U  A  H
D  I           N           E  I  S  T  C
I  R           I              R  U  E  I
U  T     F  O  S  S  E  W  A  Y     I  S  R
S  U  S  S  I  C  R  A  N           C
      R  I  V  E  R  M  E  D  W  A  Y     A
```

25   Army matters

1. Mithras, 1st century AD
2. Antonine, 37 miles
3. Ermine, 134,000 (or so!)
4. Eboracum, 9th legion
5. Cohorts, 10
6. Iceni, 2 daughters
7. Legate, 5,000
8. Standard, 60
9. Legions, 4 years
10. Tribune, 80 (originally 100)

The answer: MILECASTLE

26   Inscriptions III

1. EX VISU
2. POT (potestas)
3. IMP (imperator)
4. G
5. R (Romanus, Romani)
6. AD
7. PR (praefectus)
8. HSE (hic situs est)
9. STIP (stipendia)

The answer: EPIGRAPHS
This stone (RIB 1689) was an altar dedicated to Jupiter the best and the greatest. The letters at the end refer to the dedication being made willingly (L) to someone deserving (M), probably referring to Jupiter himself). The inscription is problematic.

27 Romanised sudoku

```
M O R D I A N E S
E A S N O M I R D
I N D R S E A M O
R M A O E N S D I
N S E I A D R O M
D I O M R S E N A
O E M A N I D S R
S D I E M R O A N
A R N S D O M I E
```

This stone (RIB 3353) was placed by soldiers of the Victorious Sixth Legion, probably as a mark of construction.

28 Wordsearch plus: who's who

Clue	Answer
Brigantian chief captured and sent to Rome	Caratacus
Emperor who died in York in AD 211	Septimius Severus
Emperor who occupied Britain in AD 43	Claudius
Emperor whose wall ran from the Solway Firth to the River Tyne	Hadrian
Empress who accompanied her husband to Britain in AD	Sabina
First governor of Roman Britain	Aulus Plautius
Governor who campaigned in northern Britain from AD 78 to 84	Agricola
Governor who suppressed a major revolt in AD 60	Suetonius Paulinus
King of the Atrebates	Commius
General who led the early invasions of 55 and 54 BC	Julius Caesar
Proclaimed emperor in York in AD 306	Constantine
Queen of the Brigantes	Cartimandua
Queen of the Iceni	Boudicca
Wife of Flavius Cerealis	Sulpicia Lepidina

```
J           A G R I C O L A
U     S U R E V E S S U I M I T P E S
L   S U E T O N I U S P A U L I N U S
I         E N I T N A T S N O C       U
U           A           B             I
S           N       C O M M I U S     D
C       I S U I T U A L P S U L U A U
A   B     A U D N A M I T R A C     A
E A           I   H A D R I A N     L
S U L P I C I A L E P I D I N A     C
A       C
R   C A R A T A C U S
```

29 Out and about in Roman Britain

```
  I   W   T I C   O
A R B E I A   U M B O
  O   L   X   P   L
A N G L E   W I D O W
I     S Q U A D   N
R A M   U   L   E G G
  B   C E R E S     A
F O C U S   S H E E P
  D   L   A   I   Y
C E L T   C O P P E R
  S   S I T   S   S
```

30 Cryptic Roman Britain

```
T R A G I C P L A Y S
O   R     I     R   E
I S C A   V   E M I T
L   H   V I A   S   T
E     V I L L A     L
T U N I C   B I B L E
S     R U R A L     M
E   N   S O N   M   E
A X E S   A   L I O N
T   R     D     L   T
S O O T H S A Y E R S
```

31 Tribal disorder

```
      A T R E B A T E S
    C O R I T A N I
      S I L U R E S
B R I G A N T E S
    O R D O V I C E S
C O R N O V I I
  D E C E A N G L I
  D U M N O N I I
  D U R O T R I G E S
    I C E N I
  P A R I S I
```

The answer: TRINOVANTES
This was the tribe from Suffolk which joined in at the outset of Boudicca's revolt.

32 Commodities

```
T I N   P O T T E R I E S
A             R         H
N     O Y S T E R S     I
N             I         P
E   W O O L   S M I T H S
R   L   V     N   U
I   W I N E   G O L D
E   V   R     O   D
S H E E P   D A T E S
```

The answer: AMPHORAE
These containers of foodstuffs, liquids and oils were essential for the import and export trade.

33 Wordsearch: towns in Latin

										D	E	V	A
	M	U	R	O	D	O	T	C	A	L		Q	
	M								M	C	U	N	
M	M	U	N	U	D	O	L	U	M	A	C	O	
U			D				I		E	L		V	V
	I			N		N		S		L		I	E
		M			I		U		L	E		O	N
M	C		A	R		L	G	L	E	V	U	M	T
A		U	O	O	L	I			T	A		A	A
D	M	R	C	R	S	U			O	A		G	S
N	C	U		A	S		R		C	T		U	I
A	A	T	I		R	T		E		E	R	S	L
L	L	U		N		O	O		V	T	E		U
O	C	P			I		B	P		U	B		R
D	A	I				D		E	I	M	A		U
N	R	A				N				T	T		M
I	I	E						O			U		
V	A								L		M	M	

34 Road numbers

P	O	R	T	W	A	Y			
P	Y	E		R	O	A	D		
S	T	A	N	E	G	A	T	E	
F	O	S	S	E		W	A	Y	
C	A	D	E	S		R	O	A	D
G	R	E	A	D		R	O	A	D
D	E	R	R	E		S	T	R	E	E	T
I	C	K	N	I	E	L	D		W	A	Y
E	R	M	I	N	E		S	T	R	E	E	T
A	K	E	M	A	N		S	T	R	E	E	T
W	A	T	L	I	N	G		S	T	R	E	E	T
D	E	V	I	L	S		H	I	G	H	W	A	Y

35 Buildings all round

P	R	A	E	T	O	R	I	U	M

The answer: PRAETORIUM
This was the commanding officer's home in a camp.
The stone (RIB 1701) was dedicated to a goddess
but as there is no name, we cannot know which
one. It was an altar.

36 Inscriptions IV

1. M (merenti)
2. EQES (eques)
3. M (miles)
4. O (optimo)
5. R
6. I
7. ANN (annos)
8. L (libens)
9. Suli

The answer: MEMORIALS
This stone (RIB 3334) was dedicated to the god
Moguns (?) and to the spirit of the place, by
someone called Lupulus.

37 Hypocaust sudoku

P	C	S	O	A	T	H	U	Y
H	A	U	Y	P	C	O	S	T
Y	O	T	S	U	H	C	P	A
C	T	H	P	S	Y	A	O	U
S	U	Y	A	C	O	T	H	P
O	P	A	T	H	U	S	Y	C
A	Y	C	U	O	S	P	T	H
U	S	P	H	T	A	Y	C	O
T	H	O	C	Y	P	U	A	S

The stone (RIB 3338) was dedicated by a man called
Longinus. It was an altar stone to DIBUS (the gods)
VETERIBUS (of old).

38 Wordsearch plus: local produce

Antenociticus head	Benwell
Birth of Mithras sculpture	Housesteads
Bronze head of Minerva	Bath
Cupid on dolphin mosaic	Fishbourne
Great dish	Mildenhall
Lion sculpture	Corbridge
Mithraic altars	Carrawburgh
Mosaic of cherub gladiators	Bignor
Shell mosaic	St Albans
Stone statue of Mars	York
Tombstone of Regina	South Shields
Venus mosaic	Rudston
Virgil mosaic	Low Ham
Writing tablets	Vindolanda

S	O	U	T	H	S	H	I	E	L	D	S	C				V	
										A						I	
F	I	S	H	B	O	U	R	N	E	R	U	D	S	T	O	N	
				E				R			B	T			D	L	
Y	M	I	L	D	E	N	H	A	L	L		A			O		
O					W						L	T	W	L			
	R					B		E			B	H	H	A			
		K		U				L			A			N			
			R	O	N	G	I	B	L		M	N		D			
	E	G	D	I	R	B	R	O	C		S		A				
	H				S	D	A	E	T	S	E	S	U	O	H		

39 Out and about in Roman Britain

	B		B		H		B		W		S	
E	R	M	I	N	E		O	N	A	G	E	R
	O		G		A	U	G		L		V	
B	U	R	N	E	D		G	A	L	L	E	Y
	G		O		S	P	Y		E		R	
C	H	A	R	M		O		I	D	E	A	L
	V		A	U	R	U	M		A			
C	H	E	S	T		T		P	I	T	C	H
	E		T		B	A	R		N		I	
S	A	B	I	N	A		A	E	S	I	C	A
	L		L		C	H	I		U		E	
S	T	R	U	C	K		S	A	L	A	R	Y
	H		S		S		E		A		O	

74

40 Cryptic Roman Britain

41 Who's in charge?

```
        P R A S U T A G U S
      C A R A T A C U S
      C U N O B E L I N
  B O U D I C C A
  C O G I D U B N U S
      D R U I D S
C A S S I V E L L A U N U S
        T O G O D U M N U S
    T I N C O M M I U S
      C A R T I M A N D U A
```

The answer: PROCURATOR
This was the official title of the governor of Britain.

42 Pointing the way

43 Wordsearch: villas in Britain

44 An L of a job

45 Help on the wall

1. Agricola, 4
2. Auxiliaries, 10 feet
3. Solway, 800
4. Birdoswald, 2
5. Irthing, 46 years old
6. Newcastle Upon Tyne, AD 122
7. Turret, 6
8. Altars, 73 miles
9. Vallum, 30 (estimate)

The answer: BATAVIANS
These were soldiers from the Rhine Delta who manned the fort at Vindolanda.

46 Inscriptions V

1. S (solvit, from VSLM)
2. II
3. LEG
4. EX
5. N (nobilissimo)
6. T
7. V (votum)
8. O (optimo)
9. I (Iovi)
10. COS
11. ET
12. S (situs, from HSE)

The answer: SILENT VOICES

The stone (RIB 1714) was dedicated to someone called Ingenuus, who was 24 years, 4 months and 7 days old. The inscription is on a tombstone, as we know from the letters DM at the top (though in fact these are missing on the original stone). It also refers to a dead person and how long he lived.

47 Cold baths sudoku

S	O	C	T	D	B	L	A	H
L	B	D	S	A	H	O	T	C
H	A	T	O	L	C	B	D	S
O	C	A	D	H	T	S	B	L
D	H	B	L	S	A	T	C	O
T	L	S	B	C	O	A	H	D
C	S	O	A	T	D	H	L	B
A	D	L	H	B	S	C	O	T
B	T	H	C	O	L	D	S	A

The mothers referred to on this stone (RIB 1692) would probably have been the mother goddesses, or earth goddesses. The stone was also dedicated to the spirit of our master, possibly meaning the emperor.

48 Wordsearch plus: galleries galore

Ashmolean Museum	Oxford
British Museum	London
Corinium Museum	Cirencester
Fitzwilliam Museum	Cambridge
Great North Museum	Newcastle
Grosvenor Museum	Chester
Hunterian Museum	Glasgow
National Roman Legion	Caerleon
Roman Army Museum	Carvoran
Roman Baths Museum	Bath
The Undercroft Museum	York
Verulamium Museum	St Albans

48 (cont'd)

C				K			R	E	T	S	E	H	C
C	I					R				L			L
A	E	R	O	X	F	O	R	D	T			O	
R	G	S	E				Y	S		N	N		
V	D	T		N			A		O	D			G
O	I	A			C	C		E	O			L	
R	R	L			W	E	L	N			A		
A	B	B		E		R	S			S			
N	M	A	N		E			T	G				
	A	N	B	A	T	H		O	E				
	C	S	C				W			R			

49 All about Roman Britain

50 Grand old Roman Britain

51   Buried in museums

M	I	L	E	S	T	O	N	E		
S	A	M	I	A	N	W	A	R	E	
		G	R	O	M	A				
		S	C	U	L	P	T	U	R	E
		L	O	R	I	C	A			
	A	M	P	H	O	R	A	E		
		C	H	I	R	H	O			
D	E	N	A	R	I	U	S			
S	T	R	I	G	I	L				
	A	U	R	E	U	S				
		S	T	I	L	U	S			

The answer: SARCOPHAGUS
This stone coffin once held a dead body. The name comes from two Greek words and originally meant *flesh-eating*.

52   Fragments sudoku

N	G	A	S	E	M	F	R	T
S	F	R	N	T	G	E	A	M
M	T	E	F	A	R	S	N	G
R	S	N	M	F	E	T	G	A
T	M	F	R	G	A	N	S	E
A	E	G	T	S	N	M	F	R
G	A	M	E	N	F	R	T	S
E	N	T	A	R	S	G	M	F
F	R	S	G	M	T	A	E	N

The inscription (RIB 1707) refers to a detachment (vexillum) of the third cohort. The animals shown are the winged horse Pegasus and a Capricorn.

53   Double trouble - battering Celts

54   Notes by numbers

S	P	A	D	E								
T	R	E	N	C	H							
T	R	O	W	E	L							
P	R	O	F	I	L	E						
C	H	R	O	N	O	L	O	G	Y			
E	X	C	A	V	A	T	I	O	N			
C	R	O	S	S	D	A	T	I	N	G		
F	I	E	L	D		N	O	T	E	S		
C	O	N	S	E	R	V	A	T	I	O	N	
M	A	G	N	E	T	O	M	E	T	R	Y	
S	T	R	A	T	I	G	R	A	P	H	Y	
S	U	R	F	A	C	E		S	U	R	V	E	Y

55   View from Rome: the thick of it

B	A	R	B	A	R	I	A	N	S		M	A	R	S
L	E	G	I	O	N	A	R	Y		E	A	G	L	E
I	N	F	A	N	T	R	Y		O	N	A	G	E	R
T	E	S	T	U	D	O		C	A	V	A	L	R	Y
A	M	B	U	S	H		P	A	L	I	S	A	D	E
S	L	I	N	G	E	R		R	A	M	P	A	R	T
B	A	L	L	I	S	T	A		C	O	H	O	R	T
A	U	X	I	L	I	A	R	Y		P	I	L	U	M
E	A	R	T	H	W	O	R	K	S		C	E	L	T

	T	H	E		A	W	F	U	L		L	I	T	T	L	E
B	R	I	T	S		C	A	N	N	O	T		T	H	R	O	W
S	P	E	A	R	S		W	H	E	N		R	I	D	I	N	G

The final answer, **The awful little Brits cannot throw spears when riding** is taken from a Vindolanda writing tablet (85.032.a).

56   Inscriptions VI

1. D (dominus)
2. E (est)
3. D (dies)
4. I (from IOM)
5. C (centum)
6. A (Aulus)
7. T (Titus)
8. I
9. O (from IOM)
10. N (noster)
11. S (senatus)

The answer: DEDICATIONS
The stone (RIB 1702) seems to name Trajan on the first line and Hadrian on the second. A lot of letters are missing but it resembles part of a marker stone from a milecastle.

57 Drill exercise

```
    L   S   D   G
  C H E S T E R H O L M
  O   G   A   I   R   E
D R U I D S   L E G A T E
  S   O   H   L   O   A
S T O N E   O   A N G L E
  O     R A D I X     W
O P E R A   E   E N V O Y
  I   E   M   S   E   R
S T A B L E   T R A C K S
  U   E   T   A   T   E
  M U L T A N G U L A R
    S   L   E   Y
```

58 Double trouble - Stonegate rebellion

```
  B   T I C   S
N E R O   R O A D
  S   W   A   L
S T O N E G A T E
P   P       C   T
A R T H R I T I C
  U   U   R   D
L I O N   O X E N
  N   T E N   S
```

```
  M   D I G   D
D I C E   A D I T
  L   R   U   D
R E B E L L I O N
O   O       L   U
W A X T A B L E T
  R   O   A   A
S C A R   T U R F
  H   C O H   S
```

59 Wordsearch plus: filling faces

beer	cervisia
bread	panis
chicken	pullus
eggs	ova
honey	mel
oil	oleum
olives	olivae
oysters	ostreae
pepper	piper
pig fat	lardum
radishes	radices
salt	sal
spices	condimenta
vinegar	acetum
wine	vinum

59 (cont'd)

```
A E A E R T S O     O
T       L       L   V     R
N     C E R V I S I A     A
E S M A M   M U N I V     D
M   U   C           A O I
I   D L   E S         L E C
D   R   L I T P I P E R   E
N   A   N U   U   U       S
O   L A S   P   M
C   P
```

60 View from Rome: a rough bunch

```
T R I N O V A N T E S   W A X
F I S H B O U R N E   Y O R K
G A L L I C W A R   B A T H S
C L A U D I U S   L O R I C A
P I C T S   S I X   S W O R D
E X E T E R   C H E S T E R S
S A X O N   L O N D I N I U M
V S L M   B I R D O S W A L D
U R N   C O N S T A N T I N E
```

```
E X P E C T   N O N E   O F   T H E M
  T O   B E   S K I L L E D   I N
M U S I C   O R   L I T E R A T U R E
```

The final answer, **Expect none of them to be skilled in music or literature** is taken from Cicero's letters to Atticus (IV.17.6).

61 Construction projects

```
          V I A
M I T H R A E U M
    C O L O N N A D E
    T H E A T R E
    B A T H H O U S E
    C O U R T
  H E A D Q U A R T E R S
  P E R I S T Y L E
      I N N
    P R A E T O R I U M
    G R A N A R Y
A M P H I T H E A T R E
  F O R U M
    T E M P L E
```

The answer: VALETUDINARIUM
This was the Latin word for a hospital.

62 Discovery sudoku

I	O	V	S	E	C	Y	R	D
S	Y	R	I	D	O	E	V	C
C	D	E	Y	V	R	S	I	O
R	S	I	C	Y	E	D	O	V
D	C	Y	R	O	V	I	S	E
V	E	O	D	S	I	C	Y	R
O	V	C	E	I	Y	R	D	S
E	I	D	V	R	S	O	C	Y
Y	R	S	O	C	D	V	E	I

The stone (RIB 1693) shows the god Mercury holding his magical staff entwined by snakes as his attendant makes a sacrifice at the altar.

63 Double trouble - Birley in urns

64 Digging in the dirt

M	I	C	K		A	S	T	O	N						
B	A	S	I	L		B	R	O	W	N					
R	O	B	I	N		B	I	R	L	E	Y				
J	O	H	N		C	L	A	Y	T	O	N				
P	H	I	L		H	A	R	D	I	N	G				
P	E	T	E	R		S	A	L	W	A	Y				
P	E	T	E	R		A	D	D	Y	M	A	N			
T	O	N	Y		R	O	B	I	N	S	O	N			
S	H	E	P	P	A	R	D		F	R	E	R	E		
T	I	M	O	T	H	Y		P	O	T	T	E	R		
M	O	R	T	I	M	E	R		W	H	E	E	L	E	R
L	I	N	D	S	A	Y		A	L	L	A	S	O	N	J	O	N	E	S

65 View from Rome: a poor outlook

H	E	R	R	I	N	G	B	O	N	E	■	R	H	O
N	O	V	I	O	M	A	G	U	S	■	O	P	U	S
H	A	R	D	K	N	O	T	T	■	D	O	V	E	R
S	T	A	L	B	A	N	S	■	L	E	G	I	O	N
V	I	C	U	S	■	A	L	A	■	I	C	E	N	I
L	I	N	D	U	M	■	A	N	G	L	E	S	E	Y
A	Q	U	A	E	■	H	Y	P	O	C	A	U	S	T
B	E	R	M	■	C	O	L	C	H	E	S	T	E	R
R	A	M	■	F	R	I	G	I	D	A	R	I	U	M

T	H	E	■	S	K	Y	■	I	S	■	G	H	A	S	T	L	Y
W	I	T	H	■	F	R	E	Q	U	E	N	T	■	R	A	I	N
S	H	O	W	E	R	S	■	A	N	D	■	C	L	O	U	D	S

The final answer, *The sky is ghastly, with frequent rain showers and clouds* is taken from Tacitus' Agricola (12).

Epigraphy Appendix

The following words or letters appear on gravestones, altars or other dedication stones found in Vindolanda. You may want to refer to them in answering the puzzles based on inscriptions. An excellent source of information on these and other Roman epigraphy can be found at https://romaninscriptionsofbritain.org/

>	from the century of
AD	to, towards
ANN (abbrev. Annos)	years
AUG	Augustus
A	Aulus
C	hundred, century (of 80 men)
CH, COH (abbrev. Cohors)	cohort
COS	Consul
D (abbrev. Dies)	days
D (abbrev. Dominus, Domini)	master
DEAE	for the goddess
DEO	for the god
DM (abbrev. Dis Manibus)	for the spirits of the departed
EQES (abbrev. Eques)	cavalryman
ET	and
EX	out of, from, according to
EX TESTAMENTO	according to the will
EX VISU	from a vision/dream
G	Gaius
GEN (IO)	for the spirit
HSE (abbrev. Hic Situs Est)	is (Est) buried (Situs) here (Hic)
I	first
II	second
IMP (abbrev. Imperator)	Emperor
IOM (abbrev. Iovi optimo Maximo)	for Jupiter (Iovi)
	the best (Optimo)

	the greatest (Maximo)
LEG (abbrev. Legio)	legion
LOC (I)	of the place
M (abbrev. Menses)	months
M (abbrev. Miles)	soldier
N (abbrev. Nobilissimo)	most noble
N (abbrev. Noster, nostri)	our
NA (abbrev. Natus, Nata)	born
NUM (abbrev. Numini)	for the spirit
OPT (abbrev. Optio)	Optio, assistant centurion
P (abbrev. Populus, Populi)	people
POS (abbrev. Posuit)	placed, set up
POT (abbrev. Potestas)	power, rank
PP (abbrev. Primus pilus)	senior centurion
PR (abbrev. Praefectus)	prefect, commander
R (abbrev. Romanus, Romani)	Roman, from Rome
R	Rufus
S (abbrev. Senatus)	Senate
STIP (abbrev. Stipendia)	years of service
SULI	for Sul/Sulis
T	Titus
TIB	Tiberius
TRIB (abbrev. Tribunus)	tribune (military rank)
	for the deserving one (Merenti)
VEXI	vexillum, a detachment
VICT (abbrev. Victrix)	victorious (name for VI legion)
VIX (abbrev. Vixit)	he/she lived
VSLM (abbrev. Votum Solvit Libens Merenti)	discharged (Solvit)
	the vow (Votum)
	happily (Libens)
VV	Valeria Victrix
	(name for XX legion)

Special note on the back cover

The writing tablet which appears on the back cover of this book was found in Vindolanda in 2017. It was written by a person called Masclus to someone called Verecundus. The section visible is a request for the return of a cleaving knife which had been loaned to Talampus from the century of Nobilis. Masclus also wrote that he had sent some plant cuttings to Verecundus. Like so many of the tablets, it's hardly great literature. Even so, their presence provides an insight into the daily lives of their writers and readers which adds enormously to our understanding of the period.

You shouldn't worry if you couldn't work any of this out for yourself. The writing tablets are fiendishly difficult to read and only real experts in the field can manage to do so.

ALSO AVAILABLE

LATIN AND GREEK PUZZLE BOOKS

These collections are aimed at those who want to have some fun with the Latin and ancient Greek languages they know and love. All of these books feature solutions at the back, for those who get stuck.

Easy Latin Puzzles was written after compiling three lists of words commonly used in a variety of Latin courses. It makes very limited use of word endings and includes a variety of challenges, including sudokus, word searches, Latin to English crosswords and English to Latin ones. The latest edition of the book has been expanded to include 60 puzzles as well as comprehensive word lists at the back.

Tricky Latin Puzzles raises the bar high for Latinists and is aimed at those who have studied the language for two or three years at least. The latest edition of the book boasts many revisions and improvements, so its 65 crossword puzzles, word-games and assorted headscratchers should bring plenty of fun.

Easy Greek Puzzles is a set of 60 brainteasers, improved and extended from the original edition, with 10 entirely new puzzles and accents incorporated for the first time. The book was first assembled from two short lists of words commonly used in a variety of beginners' courses and uses all five cases of noun, adjective and pronoun systems, as well as the active indicative verb endings from the present, imperfect, aorist and future tenses. It is appropriate for use by those who have studied the language for around one year or longer.

Tricky Greek Puzzles was written for those whose command of ancient Greek may allow them to enjoy its challenges and is definitely not for the faint-hearted. The latest version of the book has been expanded to include 65 crosswords, sudokus, wordsearches and other brainteasers and is aimed at those who have studied the language for two or three years at least.

QUARE ID FACIAM

Nil nisi latinum, nil nisi quod Cicero ipse resolvere potuisset.

Centum ludi verbis latinis in hoc libro compositi sunt in quibus gaudium et quietem e tempestate invenire possis. Inter aenigmata sunt verba transversa, favi, sagittae, coniunctis quaerendis, numeratis numerandis, novomnia, verbomnia, hodierna latinata, verba instructa.

Centum aenigmata sunt in libro sed si diligentius respicias, fortasse unum insuper videas. Si hoc aenigma CI repertum confeceris, nomen tuum in nostrum album optimatium in texto referetur.

"Si hoc intellegis...
Si lingua latina te delectat...
Si ludi cum verbis tibi oblectationem praebent...
Tibi hic liber est!"
Stephen Jenkin, The Classics Library

SONNETS FOR CLASSICAL STARS

This book was written as a follow-up companion to our earlier volume of poems, *Sonnets for Yorkshire Stars*. It contains 100 poems about leading figures in the ancient world, from the mythological to the historical, the literary to the artistic. The split in the book is roughly 50-50 Greek to Roman and the list of names included contains Poseidon, Homer, Nero and even Lesbia. The four main categories of the classical stars are Sagas and Stories, Sanctuaries and Shrines, Skill and Style and State and Standing. Highly recommended for the more poetic sort of classicist.

"Here are sonnets as history essays, as digests of the past, as mini encyclopedias and as rhyming invitations to explore further. So enjoy, and explore further!"
Ian McMillan

CLASSICAL PUZZLES

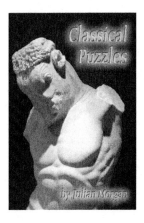

Classical Puzzles is a collection of brainteasers which focuses on the literature, culture and history of the ancient world rather than its languages. There are many people fascinated by classical civilisation who have not studied Latin and Greek and up until now, they may have been denied some fun: this book is an attempt to put that right and to complement our existing range of Latin and Greek puzzle books, not to mention the Yorkshire ones. This collection will test your knowledge of the Greeks and Romans with crosswords, sudokus and all kinds of wordgames to challenge you. Go on, test yourself out.

Can you separate your Caesars from your Ciceros? Your Spartans from your Athenians? It's all here: from art and architecture to geography, from politics to literature, from history to myths; a cornucopia of classical civilisation!

A GHOST IN THE HOUSE

Sometimes people moving into new houses can find nasty surprises when they arrive. Though sometimes the ones who were there first can find things challenging too...

Lucy has continued to stay as a ghost in the house for thirty seven years after her mysterious death. When the Mitchell family comes to live with her, she finds it very hard to like them at first. Soon, however, her new-found friend Amy helps her to uncover the lost secrets of the past and reveal why hers became such a haunting present.

A ghost in the house is a children's book, aimed at readers aged 8 and above. Despite its title, the story is not at all scary: the ghost of the title is loyal, scared, resourceful, brave, insecure and determined by turns.

IMPERIUM LATIN COURSE

The Imperium Latin course has been written for the twenty-first century; unique, highly resourced and written to make fullest use of modern technology. Its texts follow the life of the Emperor Hadrian from his early childhood to his later years, as he became the most powerful man in the Roman world.

Imperium was released for general use in 2013, after a trialling period of six years. It consists of three course books, a Grammar and Syntax book, a puzzle book and the Imperium Latin Unseens collection for advanced users. All of these texts can be ordered through Amazon but are also available as pdf files in our Site Support Packs, which can be bought by schools. The three course books are also available as free of charge downloadable pdf files, from the TES Resources website.

"Much thought and effort has gone into keeping the course rigorous and quick-paced, without overwhelming or discouraging students. The amount of assistance and supplemental material available to teachers as they present this course is truly remarkable."

Sharon Kazmierski, Classical Outlook, Fall 2013

A SERIES OF YORKSHIRE PUZZLES

  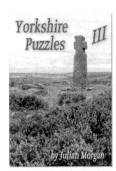

There are three books in the Yorkshire Puzzles series. Each one boasts 50 puzzles, including crosswords and other types of word-games written to test your knowledge of the county. Don't expect to find them easy unless you are an expert on Yorkshire dialect, cricket, brass bands, geography, history... and so the list goes on.

What they said about the first book in the series:

"Aimed at the more knowledgeable reader, this volume is filled with tough questions that will challenge even the most ardent Yorkshirephiles."

Dalesman, February 2017

SONNETS FOR YORKSHIRE STARS

The poems in this collection have been written to celebrate 100 of the county's outstanding achievers. The list of their names was compiled carefully to reflect all aspects of life, so you'll find artists, musicians, politicians, sporting personalities and writers here: Yorkshire's finest, all celebrated in fourteen-line verse.

"So honoured that you chose to write of me and am delighted it was in the form of a poem and not a puzzle! Warmest good wishes."

Baroness Betty Boothroyd

"Many thanks. Very interesting to read about my fellow Yorkshire folk."   Dickie Bird

"Perfectly crafted stories that brim with rhythm and dance with rhyme."   Ian McMillan

"I feel flattered to be portrayed in verse."

Peter Wright, The Yorkshire Vet

WORLD OF JAMES HERRIOT PUZZLES

Fans of the world's most famous vet, pencils at the ready! This collection was made in collaboration with the World of James Herriot in Thirsk and includes 50 puzzles, based on all eight books of the famous vet's memoirs as well as on-screen depictions, including the BBC series *All creatures great and small*.

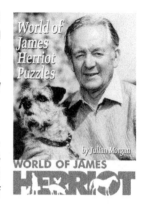

Animals and ailments, colleagues and customers, potions and powders of the original books of memoirs are all here, as well as on-screen portrayals of vets and locations, both real and fictional. Don't worry though. If it all gets too much, the solutions are in the back.

"This volume of puzzles comes from the pen of Yorkshire Author Julian Morgan and closely matches the content of the books written by James Herriot. The challenges posed vary from simple wordsearch to cryptic conundrum and will surely appeal to Herriot fans of all ages. Julian's puzzles are respectful in adhering to the original stories and will bring new ways for readers to connect again with the stories they love."

Ian Ashton, Managing Director, World of James Herriot

CITY OF YORK PUZZLES

This collection will provide hours of amusement for fans of our great county town, boasting 50 assorted crosswords and challenging word-games of various types. Facets of history, arts, attractions, streets, famous faces, sports, pubs and shops all feature, so if you love York, you should love what's on offer here.

Not for the faint-hearted, it's a good job you can find the answers in the back. So go on, how well do you know York?

ABOUT THE AUTHOR

Julian Morgan served as a teacher and a Head of Classics for many years in the UK and in Germany. Julian has now stepped down from classroom teaching and is very happy to be living in his native Yorkshire once again.

Julian has written a wide range of educational software titles and books in the last 35 years, publishing many of these under the banner of his business, J-PROGS. His Imperium Latin course is used in a good number of schools and can be downloaded free of charge by following the links from www.imperiumlatin.com. He is a member of the *O Tempora!* crossword setting team for The Times newspaper and the puzzle master for ARGO magazine.

He can often be found walking his dog in the Great Wold Valley of North Yorkshire, where he lives.

To find out more, see www.j-progs.com

Twitter feed: @imperiumlatin